Also by Anna Badkhen

Afghanistan by Donkey: One Year in a War Zone

Peace Meals: Candy-Wrapped Kalashnikovs and Other War Stories

Waiting for the Taliban: A Journey Through Northern Afghanistan

THE

WORLD

IS A CARPET

*Four Seasons
in an Afghan Village*

Anna Badkhen

RIVERHEAD BOOKS
NEW YORK

RIVERHEAD BOOKS
Published by the Penguin Group
Penguin Group (USA) LLC
375 Hudson Street, New York, New York 10014, USA

USA • Canada • UK • Ireland • Australia • New Zealand • India • South Africa • China

penguin.com

A Penguin Random House Company

Poetry by Rumi on pages vii, 130, and 174 is quoted from *The Essential Rumi*, translated by
Coleman Barks and others (HarperOne, 2004), and reprinted with permission from Coleman Barks.
Poetry by Sayd Bahodine Majrouh on pages 169 and 170 is quoted from *Songs of Love and War:
Afghan Women's Poetry*, edited by Sayd Bahodine Majrouh, translated by Marjolijn de Jager
(Other Press, 2010), and reprinted with permission from the publisher.

The Library of Congress has catalogued the Riverhead hardcover edition as follows:

Badkhen, Anna, date.
The world is a carpet : four seasons in an Afghan village / Anna Badkhen.
p.   cm
ISBN 978-1-59448-832-0 (hardback)
1. Afghanistan—Social life and customs.   2. Women—Afghanistan—Social conditions—21st century.
3. Women weavers—Afghanistan.   4. Rugs, Oriental—Afghanistan.   5. Carpets—Afghanistan.
6. Weaving—Afghanistan.   7. Badkhen, Anna, 1975–   I. Title.
DS354.B3225   2013   2013003827
305.409581—dc23

First Riverhead hardcover edition: May 2013
First Riverhead trade paperback edition: June 2014
Riverhead trade paperback ISBN: 978-1-59463-267-9

PRINTED IN THE UNITED STATES OF AMERICA

10 9 8 7 6 5 4 3 2 1

Cover design and illustration by Janet Hansen
Book design by Claire Naylon Vaccaro
Map by Meighan Cavanaugh
Illustrations by Anna Badkhen

*Unroll your carpets, and I shall see what is
written in your heart.*
TURKOMAN PROVERB

*Every moment and place says,
"Put this design in your carpet!"*
RUMI (BALKHI)

*Before man was, war waited for him.
The ultimate trade awaiting its ultimate practitioner.*
CORMAC McCARTHY

CONTENTS

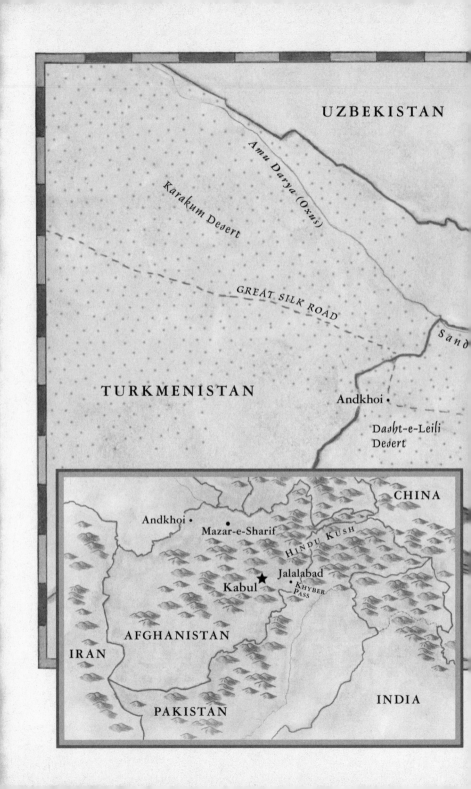

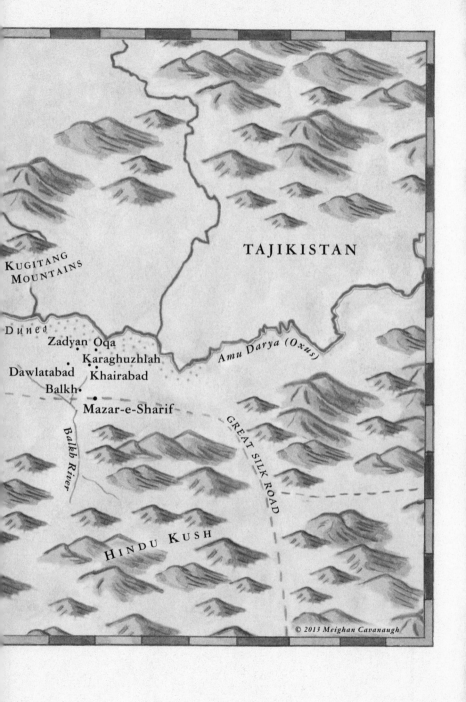

THE CARPET

At four in the morning a phalanx of black silhouettes set out across the desert: three people and a donkey headed west on a sinuous dustbowl trail. The yogurt bow of the moon had slipped behind the Earth an hour earlier, and the trail wound invisibly through thick predawn dark that arced toward the horizon. All was still. To the south, the Big Dipper scooped out the mountains I could just skylight against the spongy, star-bejeweled March night.

Amanullah led the way. He skirted the spines of cousinia and the diaphanous spheres of calligonum only he could pick out, hopped the cape hare burrows he alone knew about, sidestepped the boulders he alone remembered. He never changed pace. He never bent down to check for sheep spoor. He never looked up: he didn't navigate by stars, didn't know their names, didn't recognize the constellations. What for? Stars were unreliable beacons, nomads that moved about the heavens at will, like the Turkoman forefathers. Have you never seen one suddenly tear off from its roost and streak across the black, looking for a new home? Amanullah walked the trail by heart, steering from a memory that wasn't even his own but had double-helixed down the bloodstream of generations of men who had traveled this footpath perhaps for millennia. A memory that was the very essence of peregrination, a flawless distillation of our ancestral restlessness.

We walked single file. Amanullah first, then the donkey, then Fahim, who taught English at an evening school in Mazar-e-Sharif and was helping me with translation, then I. At a brisk clip, in dry weather, the eighteen-mile walk across the hummocked loess usually took about five hours. Amanullah had made this journey every two weeks since he was six or seven. Now he was thirty.

"If other people in the world walked as much as we do, and worked as hard as we do, they'd go crazy," he announced. He paused for effect. Amanullah bragged about the unimaginable hardships of life in the desert fondly and often. In the dark, I pictured him smile in sly satisfaction at the gravity of his own pronouncement. But when he spoke again, he sounded surprised.

"But we don't."

It was Thursday, bazaar day in Northern Afghanistan. We were walking to Dawlatabad, the market town nearest Oqa, Amanullah's village. We were going to Dawlatabad to buy carpet yarn for Amanullah's wife, Thawra.

For the next seven months, Thawra would squat on top of a horizontal loom built with two rusty lengths of iron pipe, cinder blocks, and sticks in one of Oqa's forty cob huts. Day after day, she would knot coarse weft threads over warps of thin, undyed wool, weaving the most beautiful carpet I have ever seen.

If the eastern hemisphere's carpet-weaving region that extends from China to Morocco were itself a carpet, and one were to fold it in half, Thawra's loom room would fall slightly to the right of the center fold. Prehistoric artisans upon these plains were spinning wool and plaiting it into mats as early as seven thousand years ago. Since then, people here have been born on carpets, prayed on them, slept on them, draped their tombs with them. Alexander the Great, who marched through the Khorasan in 327 BC, is said to have sent his mother, Olympias, a carpet as a souvenir from the defeated Balkh, the ancient feudal capital about twenty-five miles southwest of Oqa. For centuries, carpets were a preeminent regional export, a currency, status symbols, attachés. When Tamerlane, who was crowned emperor at Balkh, was absent from his court, visitors were permitted to kiss and pay homage to his carpet, which they were instructed to treat as his deputy.

Of all the Afghan carpets, those woven by the Turkomans are the most valued. Marco Polo, in the thirteenth century, lauded Turkoman weavers for producing "the best and handsomest carpets in the world." Six hundred years later, Francis Henry Bennett Skrine, a retired commissioner of the Indian Civil Service, and the London linguist Sir Edward Denison Ross wrote that Turkoman carpets were "unrivalled in Asia for beauty and durability." For their rich palette of reds—mahogany, terracotta, liver, and the atrorubent of the fratricidal blood that soaks their land—the Turkomans are called the Rembrandts of weaving.

Fine clay dust will filter into Thawra's mud-and-dung loom room as she weaves. Through the scrub-brush lath ceiling there will seep into the room particles of manure, infinitesimal flecks of gold from nearby barchans, the terrible black cough of her neighbors' famished children, echoes of the war that jolts the plains and contorts the

Cretaceous massifs of her land. A roadside bomb will go off, and the desert outside her doorless entryway will groan in response with the phantom footfalls of past invaders: Achaemenid and Greek, Mughal and Arab, Ottoman and Russian, British and Soviet. A speck of an American Navy F/A-18 strike fighter will catch a sudden sunray on its wing and for the instant it pierces the incredibly high azure it will become a ghost of a different glint: on Genghis Khan's sword before it split the skull of a Bactrian housewife, on the barrel of a guerrilla's *jezail* matchlock before it discharged at some subaltern of the Raj. Taliban scouts will appear on the path where Amanullah and I walked for yarn, then vanish again, the way all raiders come and vanish upon this eternal battleground.

Thawra's will be a *yusufi* carpet, a diamond pattern her mother and her mother's mother wove before her, on the backdrop of wars past. Under her thin fingers, almond-size flowers with ogival petals will shine in a field of ocher and deep maroon. Each flower will bloom from two hundred and forty knots she will tie by hand the way her foremothers did; each knot will be a temporal Möbius strip that ties past and present.

Once the carpet is finished it will take flight from this fantastically brutalized land that clings to the violent tectonics at the thirty-fourth parallel. Amanullah will roll it up and cram it into his donkey saddlebag, and his father will take the familiar footpath across the desert to deliver it to Dawlatabad. A middleman there will sell it to a dealer from Mazar-e-Sharif, the largest city in Northern Afghanistan, the modern capital of Balkh. After that, perhaps, Thawra's carpet will be jabbed into the back of a beat-up taxicab, then tossed into the bed of a truck painted with dreamy pastorals, in which it will journey across Afghanistan's war-racked landscape and over the border, through Pakistan's implacable tribal areas, to the rug markets of Peshawar and Islamabad. Or maybe it will travel west, past the mass graves of Dasht-e-Leili, across the Karakum Desert, to the bazaars of Istanbul. Or else it will trundle in the trunk of a bus bound for Kabul, from where it will fly to Dubai, and from there, across the Atlantic Ocean until it alights at a dealership in the United States, the single largest purchaser of carpets on the world market at the time of this story. A wealthy patron will pay between five and twenty thousand dollars for it. Wherever her carpet ends up, for her work Thawra will be paid less than a dollar a day.

But first, she will weave. After each knot, she will cut weft yarn from its ball with a small, sweat-darkened sickle. *Thk, thk, thk,* the sickle will go, measuring time between dawn and dusk, birth and death, peace and war, measuring life immemorial.

By quarter to six the wind had picked up. The night faded to a phantom blue, and I could see the vapor of our breath silver into pale puffs and blow away, dispersing into the hazy distances of the plains. The land turned pewter gray, dappled and tufted like a camel's hide. Warblers and larks chirped unseen on the ground. Moisture rose cold from ultramarine creases in the desert floor, and Amanullah mounted the donkey and tucked his hands into the sleeves of his faux sheepskin coat for warmth. The eastern sky blanched and stars began to blink out one by one until only Venus still pulsed, globular and dilated over the southeast. Beneath it, the Hindu Kush rose flat like an enormous theater backdrop, devoid of depth definition. A narrow, unbroken circle of pale red cirri frothed just above the horizon, as though the Earth were a furnace lid trying to contain some ineffable flame. Northwest of us, the decaying dragon's teeth of a long-vanquished, two-thousand-year-old Kushan castle mawed at the world. We passed a shepherds' shelter molded out of clay. The frassy cutbank of the Hazara Ditch that had been dry since who knows when. A tank berm from some former misbegotten war. A chunk of mortar shrapnel dinged under the donkey's hoof. From time to time, furrows crisscrossed the land where farmers from one of the bigger villages had chartered a field a long time ago, back when there had been water to irrigate the land. Amanullah rode sidesaddle across this grid and plotted his escape.

"I'm thirty years old and the only fun I've known has been fucking my wife. At least that's good. But I would like to travel someplace else before I die. Someplace more fun. I asked my father for permission to go to the city and join the army or the police. He said no. He said: 'Stay here, this is life.' After that, my father took all my money, because he doesn't trust me."

I looked at the rider. A broad man. Broomlike mustache. To keep the cold out, Amanullah had wrapped the loose end of his striped turban round his neck. Under his coat he wore a white cotton *shalwar kameez*. On his feet, a pair of slip-on shoes molded out of black rubber to look like sneakers. Even the shoelaces were molded. You got shoes like that from a heap at an Afghan bazaar, a

8

dollar a pair; when summer came, you switched to a pair of molded rubber sandals. When he was an eight-year-old grazing his camels in the sand scrub half a day's walk from Oqa, Amanullah found a rocket-propelled grenade in the barrens and put it on his campfire to see what would happen. The grenade blew up. A bit of shrapnel lodged in his left eye, and he developed a cataract and a pronounced convergent strabismus. The squint and the blemish gave him a mischievous look.

Now he was squinting northward. There, on the other side of the distant Oxus, pink tinsel of snow ribboned upon the Kugitang Mountains in Turkmenistan. Fantasies of flight welled in the waxing day.

"Once, I wanted to run away from the village and move to Turkmenistan," Amanullah mused. "The plan was to go to Turkmenistan, earn a lot of money, and spend it on the girls."

He closed his eyes.

"Girls in Turkmenistan sing beautifully."

We walked on. The donkey ambled at a four-beat gait. The earth rang hollow like a taut belly under its hooves and Amanullah began to sing to the beat. He sang sad, chromatic songs in Turkoman about the world beyond his desert, about make-believe girls who weren't his wife. He made up the words as he went. Flat quarter-tone tremolos spilled from deep inside his throat and bounced off tussocks that bristled with dry, frozen grass. Fahim whispered translations. Then the first sunray flashed tangerine above the Hindu Kush, blessing us all—humans and animals, weavers and wanderers, sinners and yet worse sinners. The planet turned to the oldest rhythm: moving and yearning.

~~~~

Afghanistan's oldest surviving minaret rose sixty stocky feet out of the plains, a stern watchman over the waking world. In the early twelfth century, Seljuk invaders had braided its tower out of pale narrow brick in the village of Zadyan, two-thirds of the way between Oqa and Dawlatabad. The clay bubble wrap of Zadyan's domed roofs stretched a mile or so to the south of the minaret, and almond groves at its foot foamed the same pink as the snowy crest of the Kugitang, as though the trees had scrounged their color from the dawn-stroked mountain range.

It was seven in the morning. Tawny arid desert yielded to swatches of startling emerald where farmers from Zadyan grew ankle-high winter wheat. On an earthwork some hundred yards to the south of the trail, three men who had been squatting now stood up and watched our procession, turning slowly with their entire torsos as we passed. Who were these men? Villagers tending their fields? Taliban scouts spying out who came and went? Bandits waiting to waylay traders headed to market with money or goods? The men did not salaam us. Amanullah heeled the donkey twice and we quickened our pace.

Amanullah steered toward the minaret. There, in the trampled clay of a large and empty square, his father, Baba Nazar, was waiting on his haunches in the slanted rays of morning.

Baba Nazar was seventy years old. I had met him a year earlier. He had been seventy years old already then. Nine months later I would ask again and he still would be seventy. Few Afghans knew how old they were: Who wanted to count the seasons of privation?

10

When he was young, Baba Nazar's mother would tell him each
year: "Now you're fifteen. Now you're sixteen. Now you're seventeen." But his mother had been dead a long time, and there was no
one to instruct Baba Nazar about his age anymore. When there was
no black left in his heart-shaped goatee, he settled on seventy. Baba
Nazar was a respected elder in Oqa and seventy seemed a good, re-
spectable number. He stuck with it.

Baba Nazar was a hunter. In a special niche of his bedroom, near
the old shotgun hanging from a nail driven into the mud wall, he
kept a pair of Soviet army binoculars with one working telescope
and a *tupcha*—a weightless, plum-size percussion he had fashioned
by hand from bird cartilage and wood and hare skin. A *tupcha* imi-
tates impeccably a quail's call that lures a covey to the hunter, but
only when it is built with the elastic skin of a freshly killed hare.

The old man had to stretch the wood-and-cartilage frame anew before each quail hunt, which meant that a hare hunt always came first. Baba Nazar hunted and trapped anything warm-blooded except for the scavenger birds that wheeled over the desert in unchallenged windblown loops. Like everyone in his starved village, he did not always have enough money to buy rice and oil. But no other family in Oqa ate meat of any kind as often as the six people under Baba Nazar's roof: the old man and his wife, the quick-faced Boston; Amanullah and Thawra; and Amanullah's small children, son Nurullah and daughter Leila.

Because Baba Nazar knew well of Amanullah's Odyssean longings, he did not trust him with the money to buy yarn for Thawra's next carpet. He was going to the market himself. But first he had to stop at a nephew's large and messy compound in Zadyan for a late breakfast of *shir roghan*, hot milk boiled with melted butter and colored pale yellow with tea leaves.

Cross-legged on a broad straw mat that covered the entire floor of a small guestroom, we crumbled fresh, hot nan into bowls of the brew and ate it, soggy, with aluminum spoons. Humus in late autumn must taste like this, I thought: mouthfuls of rich decay. A half dozen of our host's many children crowded just outside the entrance. They hid their bodies behind the wall so that only their backlit heads leaned through the door, and studied us in silence. From time to time, one of them suddenly would begin to giggle, then another, and an older child would shush and slap them, and the sniggering children would peel off from the group and disappear entirely behind the wall, then reappear moments later, still shaking with soundless laughter.

Baba Nazar and I shared a bowl. He caught me looking at the children and asked me about mine and said that it must be difficult for me to be this far away from home.

I could have told him that I did not have a home. That I was afflicted with "a longing for a home that no longer exists or has never existed," to borrow the description of nostalgia from the Harvard scholar Svetlana Boym—a longing not for a geography but a state of mind; for what Bruce Chatwin, on a quest to rationalize his wanderlust, had explained as our primordial need to remain in motion. That I had spent my adult life in motion of one sort or another in the war-wrecked hinterlands of Central Asia, Arabia, Africa. That I had been coming to Afghanistan since before American warplanes dropped their first payload on Kabul in 2001. That on my first visit, on assignment for a San Francisco newspaper, I had blacked out from malaria or dysentery or both in a dried-out tidal freshwater marsh just south of the Amu Darya, the Oxus of modern maps, of recent conflicts, of land mines and opium smugglers. When I awoke in a fluted forest of reeds, on gray sand runed by ibisbills and migrating cranes, alone, thirsty, lost, I heard, beneath the vault of the staticky stillness of a sun-scorched wasteland, the shouts of children gathering the bitter leaves of the orach plant for dinner, the crackling of a radio promising a new war, women's laughter. I heard life unyielding. And then someone, a child, was handing me a plastic water bottle. Perhaps I had come back for this: the unobstructed sky, the resilient candor of my hosts who wove joy out of sorrow, the seductive contrast between the ancient and the modern, between the unspeakable violence and the inexpressible beauty—even some dubious personal vastation that made me more alert to the intricacies of life shaped within such precarious balancing. This was the friction that pierced me the first time I saw Oqa, in 2010, when I met Baba Nazar and his family, and watched for the first time his daughter-in-law squat upon the loom. That visit had lasted an afternoon. I had to return. I had to return and spend more time here—the time it took to weave a carpet.

I could have told him what Sir Wilfred Thesiger, the British explorer, wrote in one account of his years with the Beduin of Arabia: that anyone who has stayed in places like this "will carry, however faint, the imprint of the desert, the brand which marks the nomad; and he will have within him the yearning to return, weak or insistent according to his nature." Once upon a time, we all were walking across the desert. We all carry that brand, the mark of Cain. I had been returning forever.

I could have told him all of that. Instead I told him that as a foreign correspondent I was accustomed to being away because I had been traveling, to Afghanistan and other places, since I had become an adult; that my son, who was thirteen, was used to my absences; and that he, Baba Nazar, was very kind to ask.

And all of it was true.

Baba Nazar spooned a glob of fat-pearled bread into his mouth and sucked on it for a while and pronounced: "That trail you just walked on? Even a police car cannot go there because of the Taliban. And you went on foot!"

I thought of the men we had seen in the field of winter wheat. Of Amanullah, who made the trek every fortnight to stock up on flour, and sometimes, money permitting, on oil and rice. Of millions of Afghans who journeyed on such foot-worn paths—to market; to clinics where jaded and unqualified nurses prescribed acetaminophen for any and every ailment because acetaminophen was all their pharmacies carried; to school, walking or riding their pack animals through a perpetual war that threatened the slower rhythm of their movement and dictated it at the same time.

It was possible to romanticize this land, this temporal Grand Canyon where millennia condensed in valleys between the crescents of dunes and unfurled again out of carpet knots, this seemingly organic realm where every movement was meaningful with endurance, and every step was an immense journey toward survival. It was possible to exoticize it. Then a newborn overdosed on opium. Women wailed over the slight body of a six-year-old boy mangled by a thirty-year-old land mine. Men squatted against hand-slapped mud walls and smoked cheap Korean cigarettes elaborately, as though smoking were itself an act consequential and profound, and pondered life and death in a country where war was not a marquee but a hideous and continuous sideshow that picked its victims at random.

After breakfast, Amanullah and his donkey remained in Zadyan, and Baba Nazar continued to Dawlatabad in the dark gray Toyota Corolla of the man who was working with me at the time as a driver. The hunter would have taken a taxi, one of the yellow and white jalopies that rattled villagers from Zadyan to Dawlatabad on bazaar mornings for seventy cents a person, but we had been eating *shir roghan* and had missed the last taxi out of the village.

The owner of the Corolla was a tall and lean Pashtun in his mid-forties, with a long, very black beard and long, very black hair that he combed with great and deliberate elegance into his brown *paqul* hat. He kept a wad of dip tucked under his lower lip most of the time, and he kept an ancient Luger Parabellum wrapped in a cut of brown camel wool and stashed next to the hand brake. The pistol, a German museum piece of World War I vintage, had been his grandfather's. I never saw him fire it, though I did see him cock it a few times. Everyone I knew called the man Qaqa Satar: Uncle Satar. Qaqa Satar called himself, interchangeably, Talib and bin Laden. He smoked a lot of hashish, prayed five times a day, and panicked easily and often.

There was no road, and the car rocked over tussocks and shallow dry rills scooped out by some improbable bygone rain. After about twenty minutes, a great rectangular skeleton of a fortress apparitioned out of the plains. This was Kafir Qaleh, the Castle of Infidels, built more than two thousand years ago by the Kushans—the Central Asian Buddhist nomads who had come from the east, pushed out the Greco-Bactrian descendants of Alexander the Great's army, and ruled the Khorasan for five hundred years, until the Persian Sassanid dynasty in turn overtook them in the third century. Rows of broken and sagged hemispheric roofs filled the quadrature of the castle's massive bulwark, some thirty steep feet tall, the way rows of cracked skulls fill a mass grave: dwellings, perhaps, or maybe stupas, abandoned centuries ago. Upon the wall a translucent enfilade of ancient clay battlements tapered into wind-worn stalagmitic lace that bespoke long-forgotten offensives and defeats.

Baba Nazar pointed at the crumbled crenellations with his goateed chin.

"Their enemies would come from the desert. They would fire arrows at their enemies through these slits." Deference resonated in his voice, a kind of awe that must come with having been born and grown old in perpetual crossfire. He thought awhile. "Yes. We had fighting in the past as well."

Outside Kafir Qaleh in all directions unscrolled a country where history was a progression of savageries inflicted by men with ever-evolving weapons upon the same mud-brick landscape. Archaic warriors lay in ambush here for the first time some forty thousand years ago. A few months after our pit stop, before Thawra will have woven half of her carpet, the Taliban will claim dominion over these plains. After that, who knows?

Qaqa Satar killed the engine, and the men dispersed to relieve themselves upon the millennial ruins and oxidized bits of sheep crania and shards of clay pottery: the neck of a ewer some Buddhist monk must have used to wash his hands, a wisp of discolored glaze. Their figures immediately became as small in this landscape as ants. The sun stood high now and rebated off the alkaline desert, and the whole world was white. Stiff wind smeared the domed ceramic sky with milky clouds. We reconvened atop the castle's southern wall. In the bleached plains beneath it nothing stirred.

"What do you think about this place?" I asked Baba Nazar. "Do you like it?"

I may as well have asked if he had loved his mother. For a few beats he studied me, to make sure he had heard me correctly, or else wondering what kind of a creature I was, displaced, tribeless, uncouth.

But Baba Nazar was a gracious man, and with me he was patient. He said:

"This is my country. It is beautiful."

~~~~

Most of the week Dawlatabad was a drab provincial grid of straight gray streets that shrank away behind shuttered and padlocked storefronts. But on bazaar days, Mondays and Thursdays, the whole town transformed into a great market. Men hawked pumice and dusty shriveled raisins and hubcaps and molded rubber shoes from shops and from pyramids piled on sidewalks and on the muddy medians. Men lounged on wooden platforms of *chai khanas* and kebab restaurants shrouded in veils of blue coal smoke from the grilling meat, and jumped gutters that ran green-black with rotting food to embrace one another in the ancient and ornate ceremonies of an Afghan greeting. Women in soiled white or blue burqas stopped to examine fresh lamb carcasses and cow sides, and to poke at live chickens that butchers pulled out of wire cages and slaughtered and skinned in a handful of swift strokes, as prescribed by the Koran. Men and women haggled over the price of hard pancakes of sesame-seed halwah and purplish carrots and imported children's clothes and lengths of synthetic velvet printed with fuchsia and silver flowers. Rheumy boys in flip-flops no matter the weather pushed metal carts for customers come to stock up on provisions, and amputees stared blankly from the pavement over their suppurating stumps. Donkey carts wobbled and stalled in putrid puddles. Camel caravan drivers strode down the middle of the road oblivious to the exasperated motorists who leaned and leaned on their horns, and when other motorists stepped out of their cars to watch this spectacle bad Bollywood disco gushed out of open car doors and fused all of the day's disjointed clamor into one glorious and flawless cacophony.

Baba Nazar strode with great purpose through this pandemonium. He circumnavigated a row of metal hooks displaying beef he could never afford; bounded lightly over a pile of rusty unmatched bolts arranged for sale on a piece of tarp; cut diagonally under a canvas awning stamped UNHCR, beneath which vegetable farmers were selling their produce; and ducked into a short alley. Along the western wall of the alley all the wooden double doors had been thrown open. In storage niches behind them giant skeins of yarn hung from ceilings and walls and spilled from languid piles onto earthen floors like seaweed cast up by some unknown ebbed sea. Thousands and thousands of yards of yarn: hundreds of meters of future carpets. Late-morning sun beat bright-white and sharp upon the yarn row, and the vegetable market around the corner hummed with the chatter of bargainers, but the wooly velvet of the browns and reds absorbed all light and sound. Behind each open door a quiet crepuscule reigned, as though the doors were portals to another world altogether. In the doorways men in turbans sat beside enormous sets of balance scales, each man a guard and guardian of that hushed world.

Baba Nazar's savings added up to seventy dollars in afghanis frayed with use and the sweat of many previous handlers, and he carried the money in the chest pocket of his gray cotton vest. He stood by the scale of a yarn dealer named Abdul Shakur and discussed the price of wool. Abdul Shakur sat on an old wooden trunk draped with a folded camelwool *patu* blanket and Baba Nazar stood to his left. The conversation went on for several minutes. Abdul Shakur did not offer the old man tea, a common gesture to honor a customer. Nor did he offer him a seat. There were extensive silences after each man spoke. The longer they talked, the more erect Baba Nazar stood and the smaller he appeared, more timid, vulnerable, a venerable elder shrunk to the stature of a schoolboy.

Abdul Shakur had been Baba Nazar's dealer for years. The last time Baba Nazar had purchased yarn from him, he had ended up owing Abdul Shakur some money. That had been almost a year earlier. Since then, the price of yarn had gone up by more than a third. If Baba Nazar bought enough wool for a three-by-six-meter carpet—nine feet by eighteen feet, the standard carpet size—he would end up penniless and still owing about thirty dollars. And Boston had asked him to bring back from the bazaar some carrots, onions, and potatoes.

The men conversed some more and suddenly both laughed and Baba Nazar's posture relaxed. They had come up with a solution: Thawra would weave a narrower carpet this time, a runner, only one meter wide. It takes about five and a half kilos of wool to weave one square meter of carpet; the yarn for the whole carpet would cost Baba Nazar a little more than sixty dollars. Baba Nazar reached into his vest pocket and began to count out banknotes while one of Abdul Shakur's teenage sons heaped skeins of cobalt yarn onto one dinged cup of the dealer's large scale. Upon the other cup the dealer placed two spark plugs; two smooth granite rocks, each the size of a child's head; and a rusted iron cylinder. The exact combination, the salesman and his customer agreed, that amounted to five and four-tenths of a kilo. Baba Nazar nodded, and the boy moved the yarn off the scale, dropped it on the floor, and reached back for the next color.

Over the next quarter of an hour Thawra's future carpet assembled on the floor of Abdul Shakur's shop: coils of terracotta, burgundy, beige, ocher, green, blue, asphalt. Seventeen kilos and two hundred grams in total. The dealer's boys helped stuff the yarn into a burlap sack Baba Nazar had brought in the side shirt pocket of his home-stitched corduroy *shalwar kameez*. The old man handed the dealer the money, and the two bowed to each other lightly—Abdul Shakur still seated—and wished each other that God keep them both.

In the fall, when Thawra finishes the carpet she will have woven with this yarn, Baba Nazar will bring it here, and the dealer will buy it for two hundred dollars.

Baba Nazar turned his back on the shop, twisted his black-and-white neckerchief into a rope, wrapped it around the neck of the bag, took the loose ends into both hands, and hoisted the bag onto his back. Then he shook his head once, and said:

"Expensive."

He carried the bag to Qaqa Satar's car, threw it in the trunk, untied the neckerchief, and returned to the produce row to bargain over vegetables. He was in a foul mood and bargained rudely. A few vendors shrugged at him and waved him away. At last, he bought seven kilos each of onions and carrots, piled the vegetables into the neckerchief, and tied up the four corners into a simple knot.

He didn't have any money left to buy potatoes.

W here is she from?"
      "America."
   "Where is America?"
   "This is the first time I see anyone from America. In which direction is it?"
   "It's on the other side of the world."
   It was late morning in March and the men of Oqa had gathered on a *namad* rug of camelwool felt that Baba Nazar had brought from his house and spread on the ground outside. The goats and sheep had gone to pasture with the herder at dawn, and the camels had gone to collect calligonum for kindling with the older boys soon thereafter. There was nothing to do and the men were getting some sun. They sucked on harsh filtered cigarettes and took turns pouring hot and brackish green tea into glass cups from Baba Nazar's thermos. The thermos had been made in China many years ago and was painted with three tulips, two red and one blue. The cork was friable; Baba Nazar had wrapped it in clouded plastic to keep it from crumbling into the tea. He also had brought out a synthetic Pakistani prayer rug, should anyone feel like praying, but no one did. A slight warm breeze came from the west, blowing grains of cream-colored sand and large sleepy flies and slow coils of cigarette smoke and bits of digested thorns weathered out of camel dung.
   The men had settled on the *namad* in an accustomed and age-honed sequence commensurate not so much with their age as with their stature in relation to one another. At the foot of the carpet,

facing the sun, sat Amanullah, because he was the host's son. When the tea ran out, he would be the one to go to the kitchen and ask his mother or wife to refill the thermos. Next to him squatted Naim, who was forty and still single, though in a couple of months, when his bride of three years finally turned seventeen, he at last would get married. Sayed Nafas, an old man with a beard so thin you almost could count the hairs in it, lounged between Naim and Baba Nazar. Baba Nazar himself sat at the head of the carpet near Amin Bai, whom everyone in Oqa called the Commander. Amin Bai lay on his side and chain-smoked. He was younger than Baba Nazar by a decade or two and emaciated from years of opium use and perpetual hunger. He looked like a man who did not trust others and who was not to be trusted, a man predisposed to violence. His toddler son, Amrullah, in a bonnet of green and fuchsia felt and in layers of shirts and vests home-stitched with tattered swatches of cotton and velvet and naked from the waist down, had crawled atop his father and was playing with the Commander's face, squeezing shut the man's eyes and pinching at his wrinkled forehead with translucent fingers.

Tidings of other village children ebbed and flowed. The tiny mirrors their mothers had sewn into the skullcaps of the boys and the beaded *taweez* amulets they had pinned to the lapels of the girls sparkled in the sun. The children yelled and laughed and their laughter deteriorated into the dark, sinister cough of the condemned and then rebounded again to laughter. Like a tape recording being forcibly slowed down and allowed to speed up again. Sometimes a child would run up to the rug for the men to either pinch her cheek or swat at her the way one swats at flies or simply ignore her. The men sipped their tea. Unhurried. Serene. Late mornings in Oqa could be like this.

Baba Nazar waved vaguely to the west, where the village ended and the rest of the world began. For my benefit, he and his friends spoke Farsi, not the throaty Turkoman the villagers commonly used among themselves.

"I think America is in that direction. If I know where it is, I can walk there. But I can't walk farther than Turkmenistan."

"Have you ever been inside Turkmenistan?"

"No, I only went up to the border once, when I went hunting. But never to Turkmenistan itself."

"Do you know how far Turkmenistan is?"

"No. Only that it's four days by donkey."

"You couldn't get from here to America by donkey."

"Why not?"

"Because there is an ocean between here and there."

"What's an ocean?"

"A very big river."

"If I go to Turkmenistan, there is no river, only a wall."

"How far is America?"

"Do you know how many kilometers from here to Zadyan?"

"No. About three hours."

"It's twenty-five kilometers."

"Okay."

"To America it is about ten thousand kilometers."

"So how do their soldiers get to Afghanistan?"

"They come by plane."

There was a long silence while the men considered the magnitude of such a journey. Around them the desert was laid out in late-morning haze like a boundless sheet of mother-of-pearl.

"The world is round, like a ball," I offered. "So if you go from here either way, west or east, and then get across the ocean, you'll eventually reach America."

"No," protested Baba Nazar. "America cannot be in two places at once. It has to be in only one place."

Then Amin Bai giggled and slapped his thigh with his free hand. He had been silent throughout the discourse, thinking something over or maybe lost in an opiate dream. Now he lifted baby Amrullah off his chest and gently placed him on the felt and pronounced, still laughing:

"The world is not round. It is rectangular! There is Pakistan on one end. Turkmenistan and Uzbekistan on the other end. Iran over there. The world has four corners."

The world is a carpet.

~~~

Any rug merchant in the Khorasan will tell you: two factors determine the beauty of a carpet.

One is the density of its knots. An experienced carpet dealer will count the knots by ear, running his fingernail across the hard ridges on the reverse side of the rug. The higher the pitch of the scraping sound, the finer the yarn, the closer together the knots, the longer the carpet will retain the luscious bounce of its pile. (The dealer also might fold the carpet and press on the fold. The wool of a tightly woven carpet will spring back after the rug is unfolded, leaving no sign of a crease.) Designs are plenty but which design a customer finds attractive is only a matter of taste, of subjective preference. True beauty, on the other hand, is indisputable.

The density that makes for a beautiful carpet is approximately two hundred and forty knots per square inch. This gold standard is at least as old as the oldest known carpet in the world.

It is called the Pazyryk Carpet. The Soviet archaeologist Sergei Rudenko discovered it in the late 1940s inside an Iron Age kurgan burial of Scythian nomads, where it lay encased in the Siberian permafrost of the Pazyryk Valley, which tips away from Russia's Altai Mountains toward the borders of modern Mongolia, China, and Kazakhstan. It is a pile rug two meters long and almost two meters wide. Scientists have carbon-dated it to between 500 and 400 BC.

The Pazyryk—woven with two hundred and thirty-two symmetrical knots per square inch—is indisputably beautiful. Processions of griffins, fallow deer, and horsemen in blue, red, yellow, and green wool fringe a field of lotus blossoms. The horsemen, rendered in bearded profile, closely resemble those sculpted by artisans in Achaemenid Persia, which the Scythians raided and traded with—except that in Achaemenid bas-reliefs horsemen usually walk alongside their mounts, while many of the Pazyryk equestrians sit their animals. Some anthropologists say the mounted riders indicate that the carpet had been woven not in the heart of the Achaemenid Empire but on its periphery, possibly closer to where the carpet was discovered.

Perhaps it came from the Khorasan.

Twenty-five hundred years later, in a country ransacked by the big mechanized wars of the preceding decades, a million Afghans—one out of thirty—were believed to be weaving, buying, and selling carpets; raising sheep for them; spinning and dying and trading wool for them. A timeless people in a timeless landscape keeping alive a timeless craft. Thawra in her homemade shift dress could have been squatting over the warps and wefts in any century, preserving her heritage knot by knot. Or maybe it was the other way around. Maybe it was the ancient art itself that was the guardian of life in the Khorasan and its people's keeper. Maybe, in the threadbare loom rooms of their birth, these magic carpets promised their weavers some untold salvation.

The second criterion of a carpet's beauty is as elusive and whimsical as the first is concrete. Once a dealer is done scratching and mauling the carpet to determine the density of its weave, he will flip it over and inspect the pile itself. He will not be appraising the elegance of the design. No. He will be looking for proofs of human fallibility, the prized idiosyncrasies that make each rug impossible to replicate, unique. He will be looking for mistakes.

A devout Muslim will tie a few errant knots on purpose, for a flawless design would challenge the perfection of God. Most often, however, the mistakes are unintended, accidental. They are the artisans' personal diaries.

Here the weaver ran out of burgundy yarn and switched to the cerise left over from some older weaving: the depth of color in the border changes suddenly. Here a goat ambled into the loom room and the weaver jumped up to shoo it away: the lotus flower grew an extra petal where she had forgotten the count of the knots she had already tied before she settled back to work. An ailing infant cried: a blossom is left half-finished. A neighbor walked in with the latest sex gossip from a newlyweds' bedroom—the whole village knew the groom was just a boy, so what did you expect?—and the border runs doubly thick for a centimeter or two, so busy was the weaver laughing.

The merchant will find the unfinished petal, the too-wide line along the selvage, the rhombus almost imperceptibly askew, and smack his lips, and nod, perhaps imagining for an instant which mishap could be responsible for it. He will say: "Good."

There are mistakes. The carpet truly is beautiful.

Slouched on Baba Nazar's *namad*, I thought: If the world were a carpet, then Oqa was such a mistake.

Oqa's forty doorless huts gaped at the world in a kind of hungry supplication from a low clay hummock. The hummock was shaped like a horseshoe with the heel pointing east-northeast. A convex emptiness unfurled around the village for infinite miles and curved toward the ends of the Earth. They said people had first settled on this hummock two or three hundred years ago. They said back then the desert had been a jungle of nodular black saxaul and scaly dwarf juniper and tribulus, and some Turkoman herders from Karaghu-zhlah and Khairabad, the large farming villages four hours to the south, had decided to make camp here because there had been plenty of grazing for their single-humped camels, sheep, and goats.

Perhaps this was so. But if you walked to Oqa from any direction in Amanullah's lifetime, all you saw was a dusty phantasm rising out of limitless sere plains and sand dunes beneath unending sky. If there ever had been a jungle it was long gone and there remained no trace of it. Not a single tree grew in Oqa and no trees were visible from it. The Oqans, like their nomadic ancestors, farmed nothing. The only vegetation was the thorny and nearly leafless desert shrubs and, in early spring, strange and dark glossy succulents that looked like salamanders and that seemed to appear overnight and disappear as quickly. The predominant west wind, born somewhere by the Caspian Sea and blowing almost constantly and uninterrupted across hundreds of miles of the Karakum Desert, roughed a vast sea of dunes to the north of the village and heaped drifts of sand against the western walls of Oqa's oblique adobes, as if to anchor them to the ridge, or else a sandstorm might gust them clear off the edge of the world. When the wind was strong, it blew clouds of sand and sticks and the village became an island floating in a moving sea of dust.

The few people who knew about the village called it Oq, Oqa, or Oqan. It was not on any map. Government officials in Mazar-e-Sharif told me the village didn't exist at all, under any name.

I once searched for Oqa on Google Earth, an online database that combines constantly updated satellite imagery and photographs to imitate a look at our planet from space. With a resolution of fifteen meters or fewer per pixel, it allows you to zoom in on any place in the world. You can see the taxicabs parked outside the National September 11 Memorial in Manhattan. You can see the memorial in 3-D. I typed "Oqa" in the search window and the website zoomed in on the offices of Oqa! Serviços de Comunicação in Barretos, Brazil. I typed "Mazar-e-Sharif." The virtual globe on the computer screen spun, and the dark vertebrae of the Hindu Kush fanned northward in alluvial scallops and smoothed into the cauterized Khorasan plains—and there it was, a large pointillist blotch of glaucous and gray and pale yellow against the dun backdrop the British travel writer Robert Byron had described seventy-four years earlier as "the metallic drabness of the plain." Mazar-e-Sharif, Tomb of the Saint, the capital of Northern Afghanistan. The fifteenth-century Blue Mosque looked from space like a stylized lotus flower in the center of a geometric carpet. I closed in on the treeless residential matrix of the northern working-class neighborhood where I had lived while researching this book. There was the unpaved intersection, a few blocks south of my house, where a man on a bicycle had detonated a bomb and killed three children and a grocer, leaving the septic wound of the crater to overflow forever with putrid water and rotting refuse and heartache. The grocer was the father of a teenage boy from whom I had often bought pomegranate juice. The boy had green eyes. I scrolled north a bit. There was the ivory T of my house.

I scrolled farther north, following an ecru hairline through an expanse of ocher: the unpaved track to the Oxus. To get to Oqa, you took this track for approximately forty kilometers, then ditched it at a nameless spot that absolutely no landmark designated and headed west into the desert for another fifteen kilometers or so. The tan background on the screen ran smooth along the paling road, then became reticulated into uneven quilts of sepia, caramel, mocha.

Fields of cotton, winter wheat, okra, and tobacco dealt out at random angles like playing cards. A denser scattering of cards around Khairabad and Karaghuzhlah, the villages nearest Oqa, Karaghuzhlah itself a khaki and deep green drip painting of clay roofs mingling with aisles of almonds and apricots and centennial mulberry trees. Now west, past some brown veins of irrigation canals, to the long vertical greenish double strip of Zadyan. The minaret a pale pinhead. North of here, a perfect waxen square: Kafir Qaleh. To the east, the hazel squiggle of the Hazara Ditch.

I triangulated. Oqa had to be right here, in this freckled back of beyond just south of the rippled gray surf of sand dunes and north of the last accidental swatches of desiccated fields. I zoomed in and strained at the pixels. Nothing. I zoomed in some more and the pixels blurred out of focus. Nothing at all.

If one day Oqa were blown away, or a sandstorm buried it under a barchan, hardly anyone outside would know to notice.

No roads led to the village, only herders' footpaths that each rain erased anew. Rains were rare. There was no surface water. Oqa's two hundred and forty people—knots per square inch—drew their water with yellow plastic canisters tied to lengths of rope from the two wells some previous and forgotten generation had dug by hand. The well on the southern slope of the hummock was for humans. The well on the northern slope, where the Oqans went to relieve themselves behind some large tussocks, was for the animals, but most of the villagers watered their livestock by the southern well because it was easier to make the steep downhill trek to a well only once and because anyway the water was diseased in both wells, with typhoid, cholera, and bacterial dysentery. The water in both wells was seventy-five feet beneath the surface and briny.

If you approached Oqa from the south—say, coming from Mazar or Khairabad or Karaghuzhlah—you first came to the village cemetery. All the graves were unmarked ovoids of dry clay except for one, which was confined by a mud fence. It was the grave of Baba Nazar's grandfather. Above it dangled a large ceramic jug impaled upside down on a tall wooden staff, and against the fence leaned a plywood board with three lines inscribed upon it in Arabic in dark green paint. The first line read: "In the name of God, the most compassionate and the most merciful." The second: "There is no God but God. Mohammed is His prophet." The third line was illegible, but that didn't matter, because almost no one in Oqa could read anyway—and certainly not Arabic, the language of the mullahs. No one could tell me who had put the board there.

The graves came in two sizes: big ones, for adults, and small ones, for children. Most of the graves were small. One belonged to the youngest daughter of Amin Bai, the Commander. Five belonged to the daughters of Oraz Gul and Abdul Khuddus. All of their daughters. All the children the couple had ever had.

"Every winter five or six children die," Amin Bai explained once, and the men around him echoed, in unison, like a choir in a Greek tragedy: "Every winter, five or six."

"Die of what?" I asked.

Amin Bai pulled a half-chewed Korean cigarette from his mouth, whether to better articulate his response or to think, then returned it to its notch in his thin lips. Who knew? Cold. Cholera.

Poverty. Life. All the girls in the village were named Something Gul, "Flower"—Hazar Gul, Fatma Gul, Leila Gul—the dead ones, too. In late spring, the rush skeletonweed plants that grew between the graves and on top of them sprouted bright yellow blossoms that bowed over the mounds like sharp and frigid little suns.

After the cemetery, the footpath to Oqa crabbed windward, to the northwest, then turned abruptly right, toward the village. As if those who came here were sailboats on their final tack to some spectral mooring and the path were charting their course. Or maybe to give visitors one last chance to reconsider this godforsaken destination. The first three houses at the weather tip of the ridge belonged to Baba Nazar. Two were small, single-room boxes to keep newborn kid goats in early spring and to host the occasional houseguests in all other seasons; the main house was slightly larger, with three rooms and a kitchen and a woozy entryway on the lee side, and sat a bit farther inside the village boundary. There were no fences around Baba Nazar's houses or, for that matter, around anyone else's: privacy, vigorously guarded by thick compound walls in most of Afghanistan, meant little here. Oqa's women walked through the village unveiled, and nursed their children in plain sight.

Baba Nazar had sculpted his houses out of the desert by hand, and their walls were lumpy, like claymation props. A jerry can with the words TURBO ACTIVE ENGINE OIL fading from its side hung from a knobbly rafter outside the larger house, where the hunter and his family lived. In the late nineties, when Baba Nazar's older daughter, Zarifshah Bibi, was a teenager, she was playing under this rafter and tripped a Soviet land mine that had been buried in the dust. The explosion tore off her left leg below the knee and her left thumb, index, and middle fingers. Baba Nazar still managed to find a match for her, a sharecropper from Zadyan named Mustafa, who was in his fifties when they married. Mustafa had little money to pay the bride price. His few teeth were stained brown from chewing *naswar*—a blend of tobacco leaves, calcium oxide, and wood ash— and never brushing. He was the man you married when you had one leg and a hand with fingers missing, a hand that couldn't weave.

On the opposite, leeward end of Oqa stood the teetering shanty of the village mosque. The villagers themselves had hand-molded the mosque out of brush and mud. It had no minaret from which to summon the faithful to prayer, no arched mihrab, no calligraphy over the door. It offered no succor. Once, the Oqans had hired a mullah to come by motorcycle from the silty banks of the Amu Darya and lead them in prayer on Fridays. After a few months the mullah quit, no longer satisfied with the two hundred and twenty dollars a year the villagers could scrape together to pay him. The Oqans were left to pray alone, in the crepuscule of their homes or outside, kneeling west-southwest on kerchiefs or prayer rugs they spread over drying goat turds.

Oqa did have one building with sharp corners and straight walls. It was the shelter for a twenty-three-horsepower generator made in China by Shandong Laidong Internal Combustion Engine Co. Ltd. A few years after the Americans had come to Afghanistan, some Afghan men showed up at the village in pickup trucks, delivered the generator, filled it with fuel, built the shelter for it, raised twelve aluminum poles, ran a power line between them, and left. The power line sagged from pole to pole the curved length of the village. It was not hooked up to any of the houses or to the generator, and there were no streetlamps or electric outlets anywhere. Just as well. For two nights after the generator arrived, the villagers ran the motor from dusk till sunup, to see how much it would cost to operate it. Then the fuel ran out. The men of Oqa figured that each family would need to pay twenty cents per night for gas. Then they gathered up the wires that would have connected the generator to the power line and gave them to a villager named Choreh for safekeeping, presumably until such a time when the Oqans strike it rich. Village children used the poles for target practice with their slingshots. Whenever they hit one, it pealed magnificently, like a bell.

Three years after the generator arrived in Oqa, two foreign men came by car every day for twenty days with cameras and filmed something. No one here quite knew who these men were or what they had come to film or why. Some villagers believed they were British. Journalists documenting the opium addiction that plagued the village? Geologists cutting for sign of some rare mineral that could be extricated from the dunes should the war ever abate? Scholars looking for the graves of the fabled Great Game player William Moorcroft and his companions, George Guthrie and George Trebeck, who met their end somewhere in the Bactrian plains? Or the Britons' latter-day successors, NATO scouts? After twenty days, the men stopped coming. No one in Oqa saw them again.

"The Soviets were in Afghanistan. They passed through Oqa. The mujaheddin passed through, too—like Ustad Atta, who is now the governor. The Taliban also passed through. Everyone passes through Oqa. No one stays. It's a forgotten world."

Baba Nazar spoke, and on his *namad* the other men nodded and contemplated in silence a universe that chose to trespass on their village in such warped, distorted ways, as though reflected in a carnival mirror. It was noon. A lustrous morning had temporarily returned shape to the formless objects of the night, but the high sun had flattened them out again into two-dimensional and nebulous apparitions. The Hindu Kush became a long mauve smudge crudely smeared over the southern horizon. Out of refracted desert two enormous camels loaded with mountains of calligonum sailed on stilts without touching the ground, shrinking as they approached. A few minutes later, Amin Bai's firstborn, Ismatullah, fourteen and solemn, came and knelt quietly on the ground beside his father. The boy had gone with the camels to gather the brush, which he would barter as kindling for rice, salt, flour, tea, and cooking oil in Karaghuzhlah or Khairabad. Until the Americans came to Afghanistan, the Oqans had taken calligonum all the way to Mazar-e-Sharif, a seven-hour walk to the south, where people were wealthier and the brush sold for more. But the American war had made people in cities wealthier still, and now Mazar was full of cars. A few cars would have been okay, but this many cars scared the camels, made them skitter. A city car could hit a camel. It was not worth it to walk all the way down there anymore.

On top of that, for two years running there had been no rain. Prolonged cyclical droughts had sapped the desert since anyone could remember, but lately the droughts seemed to last longer and the cycles were more frequent. What if calligonum ran out?

"It's not like there's a jungle out there," worried Amanullah. "Day after day there is less of it. One day it will be finished. Then we'll sell all our animals—donkeys, camels, goats—and go to Mazar and look for city work there."

For all his dreams of running right off the margins of his rectangular world, Amanullah dreaded that day.

"When I go to the city, I get a headache because there is a lot of traffic, noise, pollution. Here it's very quiet."

"Yes, it is so quiet," said Sayed Nafas. The older men had listened to Amanullah speak and had nodded their acquiescence to his worries, but now they were glad for the opportunity to change the subject to something good on such a peaceful day and pitched in eagerly.

"At night you can see stars everywhere."

"It's gorgeous."

"You really should see it."

Suddenly something startled a brace of ducks out of a hollow by the cemetery. The birds flowed in long streaks over the desert, all wings and necks; circled twice, as though unable to find their vees at first; then headed southeast, black and perfect against the golden sky. Baba Nazar followed the birds with a hunter's appraising gaze. Then he announced that Thawra would begin to weave the carpet on Friday. Friday was an auspicious day to start a carpet because it was a holy day. The carpet would be blessed.

～～～

B ut first something had to be done about the loom room roof. Once upon a time, Turkoman pastoralists lived in portable *kibitkas*, semiorbicular yurts they raised with bentwood frames and homemade felt wherever they found pasture. In the winter, the *kibitka* would center around a hearth, and in the warm months, around a loom. Now most Bactrian Turkomans lived in stationary homes of desert clay, as permanent as permanence was conceivable in these volatile plains, though the women still found it too cold to weave in winter. Thawra's loom room was a groggy lean-to of the selfsame clay appended to the leeward side of the main house. From November to March, Baba Nazar's family used the room to store calligonum feed for their two camels and their donkey, and to keep their nanny goats.

The room's two entrances, one from the main house and one from outside, seemed sawed out of the walls by a three-year-old with pinking shears. There was a single door, chest-high and pieced together from five unvarnished and imprecise two-by-fours. The door was not attached to any frame. In the warm months, Thawra would lean it interchangeably against one of the entrances, depending on which part of her world she wanted to keep out the most at a given moment. In late fall, she would use the door to screen off entry from the house, and Baba Nazar and Amanullah would mortar the other entryway with fistfuls of moistened clay, which they would bash in when the weather became warm again. They did the same with many of the glassless windows in the house. One time in early May, when we were sipping tea on narrow tick mattresses in Amanullah's bedroom, the old man suddenly rose to his feet and punted at the wall. Clumps of dry clay rattled onto the stained ticking and pulverized clay flew everywhere. A window materialized at knee level and instantly there was a pleasant breeze. The other people in the room seemed not to have noticed, and sipped their tea through a film of fine dust. As if the hunter had cracked open a casement, or drawn the drapes.

The loom room had been roofed with withered bouquets of desert brush that rested upon four knurled and ancient tree trunks. This was shoddy work even for Oqa. Most roofs in the village were roofs of lath and clay, straw-mat roofs, roofs of solid adobe smeared over poplar beams, which had to be brought by camel from Karaghuzhlah or Khairabad, the nearest settlements where trees grew. Even before it caved in, the roof of Thawra's loom room had looked like an upside-down desert, tussocked and unreliable. Then, in the fall, termites ate through one of the central rafters. One afternoon straw and sticks and frass poured onto the loom upon which Thawra and Boston were knotting the last inches of a large *yusufi*, nine by eighteen feet. The women ran out of the room before the beam collapsed into it. The carpet was undamaged, and Thawra finished weaving it without a roof. It sold for more than three hundred dollars. The one good thing about the drought, Baba Nazar observed, was that it didn't rain upon the carpet.

There was always hope that the drought would break, though. The day before Thawra was to start weaving, Amanullah set out to perform roof triage with a length of gray plastic tarp and twenty-five meters of rope.

He climbed upon the wall and spread the tarpaulin over the mutilated loom room and paid out enough rope to string through the metal loops in the edging and then some. He tied the excess rope around the rafters that still lay in place over the corners of the room and tied rocks the size of a sheep's head to three ends of the rope to weigh down the waterproof sheeting. Then he jumped down and dug out of a pile of kindling a corroded mortar shell casing and filled it with smaller rocks and clods of clay and packed those in with his knuckles. He tied the shell casing to the fourth end of the rope and scrambled up onto the wall again to adjust the tarp.

Amanullah worked and bragged about how hard he worked.

"How old are you?"

"Thirty-five." I was on the ground, pulling taut a slack length of rope.

"Ha! You see these wrinkles?"

I saw.

"If you work as hard as me for six months, you will become old like me. It will only take you six months."

He thought about it.

"By the time I'm thirty-five, I won't be able to walk, even."

He thought about it some more, knelt to adjust the shell casing, then straightened up.

"By the time I'm thirty-five, I'll be dead!"

Satisfied with this awesome augury, he began to fantasize about how he would fix the roof for real one day. He would bring the wood from Mazar-e-Sharif by *zaranj* motor-rickshaw and draw water from the well and mix it with clay and build a new roof. No: he would build a whole new house! No: he would sell the camels and build a new house not in Oqa but in Karaghuzhlah, where there was an irrigation ditch to water the orchards that grew the sweetest peaches you had ever tasted and almonds so milky they melted on your tongue. Amanullah stomped around, juggling bits of rotten beam and coils of rope. A dreaming man aloft in his reverie against a lapis-blue sky. The clay walls gave dangerously underfoot.

Baba Nazar rode his donkey out of the desert. He wore a pair of glasses he had tied to his head with a soiled string because one of the bows was missing, and rubber loafers gray with dust and mud over bare feet, and he had crammed his shotgun barrel-up into one pannier of the saddlebag Boston had woven for him out of scratchy undyed wool. In the other pannier were two dead desert doves. The hunter rode up to the house and sat the donkey and squinted askance at his son balancing on the roof. The ersatz gymnast. A prairie dog popped out of a burrow on the southern slope of the hummock and froze, watching also. On the other side of the house, Amanullah's daughter, Leila, a four-year-old pixie with a blueblack pixie hairdo, made tinier still by her older brother's hand-me-down *shalwar kameez*, ran small circles around an electric pole. She held on to the aluminum shaft with one hand and held the other hand outstretched for balance and sang: "I'm turning I'm turning I'm turning I'm turning I'm turning I'm turning I'm turning I'mturning i'mturningi'mturning!" And then she sang: "I'm dizzy I'm dizzy I'm dizzy I'm dizzy I'm dizzy I'm dizzy!" An apprentice dervish whirling in an inexpert *zikr* in the desert of Rumi's own birth. Or any four-year-old girl, anywhere in the world.

~~~

I had planned to spend the night in the loom room. I was staying that year in the working-class residential neighborhood of Mazar-e-Sharif called Dasht-e-Shor, the Salt Flats, a treeless unpaved grid

41

on the northern edge of the city where alkaline soil yielded brackish water and boys' simple kites and white doves somersaulted with one another at dusk, and where I was renting an echoey room in a new house of poured concrete that belonged to a large Tajik family. Mazar-e-Sharif was the third most populated city in Afghanistan, but the wide sheetmetal gate and the tall concrete fence around the house accorded my hosts and me an illusion of privacy, of confidentiality, of protection from those who believed that a Western woman had no business living in their city and that an Afghan family had no business hosting her. In reality, everybody on the street knew where I lived, and probably everybody in Dasht-e-Shor as well, because in Afghanistan everybody knew everything. There was a south-facing and untiled deck on the second floor where women sometimes slept on the hottest nights of summer, and there I would stand and drink tea and watch the Hindu Kush, ten miles or so to the south, texture fifteen thousand staggered feet out of the blackness before dawn and light up tangerine and coral at sunup and flatten out in the hazy daylight and regain its dizzying dimensions before fading to black again at night. I would watch, between the deck and the mountains, the whole of the city wake, pray, work; watch construction workers lay by hand the pale clay bricks handpressed and fired in desert kilns halfway between Mazar and Oqa; watch ragpickers push their wooden barrows through unpaved streets; watch white doves cloud over the Blue Mosque whose domes I could not see behind an enfilade of Communist-era high-rises downtown; watch the children of my hosts hose the patio at noon to keep the dust down. And who watched me?

My rental room faced a neighbor's cowshed where a single bony milch cow sighed meaningfully in her sleep and whipped her sides with the rope of her tail, and each swish sent into my window the comforting smell of manure and deputations of large flies that shone like new buttons. The room had a tick mattress on the floor over-spread wall-to-wall with a factory-made maroon carpet, and it had heavy curtains of beige polyester, and occasionally, it had electricity in a single wall socket. Into this room at all hours of the day filed the hosts' many children with requests for pencils and offers of im-promptu Farsi lessons, women with gifts of dried fruit and laments about men, men with questions about fidelity and sex, the occa-sional houseguest wishing to greet the awkward foreigner in per-son. From this room I traveled the Khorasan, sometimes for days at a time.

But when I said I would like to stay in Oqa for the night, Qaqa Satar cried and swore I would be kidnapped by bandits and climbed into the car and started the motor, and although Baba Nazar and Amanullah and Amin Bai promised I would be safe in their village and I believed them, that evening we drove to Karaghuzhlah.

The world was a Nicholas Roerich fantasy. Harsh daylight had softened to a silky orangeade dusk. The desert had turned straw-berry and fluffed in the south into the pink wedding cake of the Hindu Kush, and the sky was lavender. A pair of emaciated foxes trotted across the plain, one slightly behind the other. Qaqa Satar leaned out the window and took aim at the animals with a make-believe gun. *"Pau! Pau!"* The foxes stopped and turned, and the one in the lead sat down and pointed his triangular face at our car and his pale amber eyes watched us pass.

It was night by the time we reached the big village. Invisible roosters screeched farewells to a sun long gone and in the east a chrome perigee moon rose and threw sharp and wicked black shadows upon angled blue streets. The streets were empty and narrow and unlit but for the moon, and after a few labyrinthine turns I lost track of our route.

Our host was Naushir, Qaqa Satar's cousin, a beautiful man of about fifty with the narrow face of a candle-blackened Byzantine saint. Naushir was a detective in the Afghan border police and the husband of two wives. When his sons dragged open the tall wooden gate of his compound to let Qaqa Satar park his car inside, Naushir stood in the middle of his yard, dressed impeccably in an ivory-colored camelwool *paqul* hat and matching *shalwar kameez* and vest, tall, smiling in the headlights. The men embraced: a slap on the back, three kisses, an excited incantation of Pashto greetings. Naushir shook my hand with both of his, "Welcome, welcome," and bowed us into the house. A guest from afar was always received warmly because such a guest was a storyteller, a griot, an entertainer to take the host's mind off the drudgery of life in a war zone.

Upstairs, a single convulsing lightbulb fed by a neighbor's generator illuminated a long room. In the corner a sheet-iron *bukhari* stove smoked through half a dozen poorly soldered seams, and a giant galvanized kettle boiled on top. Naushir, who had been an army officer for twenty years before joining the police force, reclined on a tick mattress draped with a burgundy and black carpet and exuded martial control. His three teenage sons wore *shalwar kameez* of identical bathroom-tile blue cotton, like uniforms. They hung on his every word, rose when he did, and rose also whenever he entered the room. Wordlessly they knelt before each of us with terrycloth towels, soap, and pewter pitchers of warm water while we washed our hands before dinner over ornate basins they also had brought. Wordlessly they spread a plastic *dastarkhan* on the floor and served us food and tea, then settled by the door in a formation just as silent. They did not eat.

We supped on *lobio* of stewed red beans and nan and chicken thighs Naushir's wives had deep-fried in canola oil until the tough meat had turned translucent and shrunk almost entirely from the bone. After dinner, one of the boys took me to the women's half of the house to meet the wives. They had been drinking tea in a very warm room that smelled of babies and profound sadness. One of the wives looked very old, the other very young; they could have been grandmother and granddaughter. Both were extremely thin. They greeted me with earnest kisses and clawed, anguished embraces. As though I had brought with me some salvation, some remedy for heartbreak. But I spoke no Pashto and they spoke no Farsi, and I had nothing to offer except for awkward silence. "Forgive me," I said. I don't know if they understood my apology, or even for what I was expressing regret. For intruding upon their unhappiness? A few minutes later the boy escorted me back to the guestroom where the men were sipping tea and talking. I never saw the women again.

Naushir was a good conversationalist. He brought out his AK-74, which, he pointed out with some pride, was Russian-made and not one of the imports from China or Serbia, which were more common in Afghanistan and which were considered inferior rifles. We discussed the history of the automatic weapon and of its Soviet creator, Mikhail Kalashnikov. We talked about how Naushir needed to carry the gun for personal protection when he rode his motorcycle to and from work in Mazar-e-Sharif, because Taliban insurgents were threatening to kill Afghans who worked for the government. We talked about how ten years after American soldiers had entered Afghanistan, things in Afghanistan were not improving.

"We have more of something than ten years ago," he offered. "Corruption."

After tea, Naushir and Qaqa Satar took turns praying by the stove. Then they rolled a joint and played a card game I couldn't follow. Naushir's brother, who had arrived during tea, joined neither in prayer nor in debauchery. His name was Shir Mohammad. He had been teaching Pashto in Karaghuzhlah's high school for boys for thirty years. In the Khorasan that seemed both a long time and no time at all. We talked about that. We talked about the conceit that Afghanistan exists outside time. It was true that the rhythm of life here may have remained unchanged for millennia, the seasons doled out in forever-repeating segments of lambing and fasting, of lavish weddings and meager harvests and raids by foreign invaders. All were expected here in equal measure, like the passing of time itself. But the subtlest alterations, barely perceptible and seemingly superficial to an outsider—those were truly significant because they bespoke real, existential changes to the substance of the land. "Take, for example, the high school students," said the teacher. "They are no longer bringing their Kalashnikovs to class, like they did before the Taliban. And they are worldlier. They watch different TV programs and so are more exposed to the world. Many of them have been to other countries."

Of course they had. Since the Soviet invasion in 1979, some six million people—a fifth of Afghanistan's population, and the world's single largest refugee group for decades—had fled abroad, mostly to shantytowns in Pakistan and Iran. Two generations of Afghans had been born in these refugee camps: embittered, indoctrinated by itinerant mullahs, radicalized by poverty and the rightlessness of exile. Shir Mohammad's students were the second generation.

Hashish smoke mingled with smoke from the dying *bukhari*. The men switched to Pashto and the world became woozy. Qaqa Satar interrupted the game and took me up some steps to the flat clay rooftop of his cousin's house. It was very cold and very quiet. A lidded moon branded the night. Below, beneath the pewter sheen of moonlit rooftops quaked a few lights from gas lamps and electric lamps fed by unsteady generator current. Mostly, the village was dark. The Milky Way trawled her dazzling entourage east to west. A few months later, at a conference in faraway Austin, Texas, astronomers would announce that they had deduced the exact color of our galaxy. It was, they said, the color of new spring snow an hour after dawn.

I shivered and swayed uncertainly in this vast and gelid universe.

"Aim for the waterspout," instructed Qaqa Satar. Then he went inside and left me to squat between the village and the sky.

When I returned to the room, the *bukhari* had stopped burning, the light had gone out, and the card game was over. The men were talking in whispers and I went to sleep fully dressed. The last thing I saw as I drifted off was Naushir standing above my mattress by the window. He was gently spreading an extra blanket over me: an impromptu act of kindness, simple and immense.

~~~~

The first thread was white. A four-year-old girl strung it on a Friday.

Holding a ball of undyed yarn with both hands, Leila stood over a corroded iron pipe that rested on a pair of cinder blocks along the southern wall of the loom room. She bent down and, switching the ball from one hand to the other, hooked the yarn under the pipe. Simple sorcery: just like that, the pipe became the bottom beam of a horizontal loom. The weaving will begin here. Leila pivoted around elaborately and ran across the earthen floor strewn with goat droppings and chicken feathers and straw. She stopped at the pipe in the opposite end of the room—the top beam—and looped the yarn over it. With the great ceremony four-year-old girls can be so good at. Her face solemn. Her palms sticky and pinkstained with sugar candy. She ran back: under the beam the thread went. Up again: over the beam. The yarn crisscrossed halfway between the two pipes, marking the center of the future carpet. Back again. Up again, and then back, and up, and back, and up, and oops—she dropped the ball and it rolled askew on the floor and the yarn dragged through drying bird shit and dust and God knows what else and Leila dashed to pick it up and kept running, from the bottom of the loom to the top, eighteen feet there and eighteen feet back, up and down, back and forth, I'm turning I'm turning I'm turning I'm turning I'm turning I'm dizzy I'm dizzy I'm dizzy!

"Good girl!"

"Don't you drop that thread again!"

"A bit tighter here, Leila *jan*!"

"Keep going!"

Amanullah and Boston squatted at either end of the loom and slid plywood chips between the pipes and the cinder blocks to adjust the beams' height and level while Leila shuttled between them. Boston cheered on her granddaughter and laughed and uttered instructions and pushed the warps on the upper beam closer together with her fingertips. I asked her how many warp threads there had to be to weave a meter-wide carpet, how many times Leila had to shuttle between the beams. She said she never had counted them. She only knew what the warps must look like, feel like, remembered the density of them on the loom.

Even when Boston was at rest she never was completely still. The small dark stars of her eyes leapt from one object to the next constantly to assess what else needed to be done. As if not just her spartan household and her rambunctious grandchildren but the entire world required her looking after it. Her face was an ever-revised cuneiform tablet of deep lines that wrinkled and smoothed out and refolded in a new direction every instant like the surface of a windswept lake. Her thin gray braids, which fell to where her threadbare cotton dress was beginning to rip over her saggy chest, trembled lightly with each heartbeat. Around her neck she wore a ring of keys on a thin rope, like a necklace. Her name, in Turkoman, meant "garden." She was in her sixties. She called me her older sister.

Amanullah's roof sutures hadn't lasted and the tarp was gone. Some boys perched on the eastern wall of the loom room, looking in, and rained granules of clay onto the warp. From time to time Amanullah would look up—"Scram!"—and the boys would duck halfheartedly in response and more clay would fall. Somewhere outside a hysterical donkey brayed. Above the boys a light gale blew tight white cumuli across a hard winter sky, and the light in the room flickered as the clouds raced past the sun. I wondered what the room must have looked like from up there. Leila's bone-white loom itself a tiny floccus cloud gathering in the middle of a dun desert. A pale open palm offering up her singsong, her father's ineffective scolding, her grandmother's quick chuckles, the room marbled with shadows and light, the donkey's bellows, the goat droppings, the clay dust—all that out of which a carpet was becoming.

Do you own a carpet? Touch it. Feel for the sticky palm prints of a little girl on the warp.

⌇⌇⌇

Later that morning Thawra stood up from a ceramic basinful of laundry in Boston's bedroom, stretched, wiped her hands on the sequined and sun-faded front of her frock, and entered the roofless loom room.

At the bottom beam, the woman, tall and reedthin in her shapeless calico, paused to adjust her flowered headscarf where it tied at the nape. Then she shook off her rubber flip-flops one by one and stepped in her bare feet upon the wefts her daughter had strung taut like zither strings. In a loose and single downward motion like a marionette collapsing, she squatted, facing north. Facing the top of the loom. Facing the end of a carpet not yet begun but already richly complete in her prescient mind's eye: *maida gul*, little flowers, liver red and blue of the utmost dusk strewn around the tawny field. An unintentional stylization of Oqa with its harlequin children dashing about the dusty hummock outside in frenzied tintinnabulations.

Thawra leaned forward and reached for a ball of weft. Plucking the strung wool like a harpist, she ran the end of a burgundy pile thread all the way around two warps, pulled on it, and, with a sickle, cut the weft an inch from the warp. Textile experts call this type of knot "Turkish," "symmetrical," or "double." Thawra knew no such appellations. She just tied thread over thread, making the first of one million one hundred and sixteen thousand knots. Each one protozoan, irreplaceable. And again. And again. And again. Deft, precise, rhythmical, re-creating a design that had been passed on for generations unnumbered. Yet Thawra's carpet, like each carpet ever woven by a woman's hand, will be subtly different. It will be hers alone: her future autobiography, her diary of a year, her winter count, with its sorrowful zigzags, its daydreamy curlicues, loops of melancholy, knots of joy.

There was something else, too. (This was a secret, and the weaver's thin lips curved thinner still with a discreet and private smile. Not even Amanullah knew.) The bottom sixth of her carpet will be almost imperceptibly queasy, a two-foot-long chronicle of morning sickness. Thawra was two months pregnant with her third child.

Thk, thk, thk, Thawra's sickle kept time with not one heartbeat, but two.

In the afternoon Amanullah joined his friend Asad for a walk in the dunes.

The dunes lapped at Oqa's northern slope. They were the southernmost margin of a barchan belt that extended two hundred miles west to east along the left bank of the Amu Darya and covered an area about the size of Connecticut. At Oqa, which marked roughly the middle of this vast colony, the sands were approximately twenty miles wide and the color of tea with milk. If one were to cross the dunes here—it would take three days by camel, and there would be no wells along the way—one would come to a village called Dali. You couldn't see even half that far in the dunes, of course. You couldn't see even half a mile. But what you saw was enough to get the feeling that the sands were neverending.

They had no formal name. International relief agencies called them the sand dunes in the Amu Darya Valley, the Amu Darya Desert, or the Shor Teppeh Desert. The Oqans called the dunes *dasht*, desert. They called everything around the village *dasht*. In a way, everything was. *Dasht* was the ultimate life-force that giveth and taketh away, a modus operandi, a state of mind.

The barchans were made of billions of tons of sand the wind constantly herded east from the Karakum Desert. Some of the grains had journeyed through these plains at least once already, when the Amu Darya had carried them west from the Pamir and the Himalayas through the Hindu Kush. Dust from the roof of the world. Central Asia's last true nomads. Now they were returning, slow but indomitable, curved into enormous and infinitely precise swords and crescents, caressed into minute ripples and crinkles, razored into perfect crystal-thin crest lines. A surrealist masterpiece of sand. Splayed out and aquiver like a lover of some epic and unknowable god in a phantasmagorical foreplay. Sand slithered over itself in airborne slipstreams that drifted several inches off the ground, continuous, serpentine, defying gravity. Defying everything. Weightless and leaden at once. Grain by unstoppable grain it crept up windward slopes fifty feet high and then cascaded down concave slip faces like tendrils or tentacles forever reaching eastward. The slow-motion undulation triggered vertigo. If you sat on a dune for a long time you could feel the desert move. In some parts of the belt, the dunes migrated three feet a day, smothering oases, roads, villages. The jungle that had seduced Oqa's founding fathers lay buried somewhere below.

Amanullah removed his shoes and walked along the crest lines. Wind blew sand against his bare ankles and he sang guttural songs that had no words but had everything else: the spilled-yogurt moon, the donkey ride across the hollow tabla of the desert, the neon explosion of sunrise, his little daughter building the perfect and simple geometry of a carpet loom. An ageless man tracing the liminal with his bare feet beneath that Georgia O'Keeffe sky. Then he winked at me, plopped down on the sand, and slid down the slip side of a dune on his ass, shoes in hand. When he landed at the ruffled bottom he laughed and informed me that the dunes were made of gold.

And they probably were.

A year earlier, the United States had announced that a team of Pentagon officials and American geologists had discovered nearly a trillion dollars in untapped mineral deposits in Afghanistan—including, potentially, twenty-five billion dollars in gold. It would take years, maybe decades, to establish proper quarries to mine these resources on an industrial level, war permitting. But I had seen years before, in the muddy and cold rapids of the Amu Darya, men in rolled-up pantaloons sifting the sand through pans, bedraggled and desperate prospectors. Amanullah sat down and held forth a handful of sand and I saw, in his palm, golden specks.

"Can you imagine that we might be literally living on gold?"

Why not? That year, Nigeria was sitting on thirty-seven billion barrels of proven oil reserves and eight out of ten Nigerians were living on less than two dollars a day.

"If we had special machines, we could get gold out of this and get rich. But we are too poor to buy such machines."

And again Amanullah schemed a breakout. He would sift the dunes for gold and become a millionaire and buy a nice house and a car somewhere far away, where water and girls were plenty. He would join the army and learn to read and write. He would find a job as a day laborer in Mazar, learn to sleep through city din. He would get away. He would. He would.

This man, whose dreamy wanderlust echoed my own, whose rough and earnest embraces greeted me each time I arrived in his village, whose love of corporeal life was as exuberant as his living was meager. I liked him immensely. I took off my shoes and skidded to where he sat and lay down beneath a dune and listened. The gale had risen to thirty knots and effaced the anvil clouds from the sky and effaced the history of violence from the dunes, or at least ploughed it under. It carried sand, children's voices, the rustle of desert grass. It carried echoes of wars ancient and recent. It carried terrible and inexplicable yearnings, for a future that was improbable and a past that never had been. It carried nostalgia. Time fell away.

Then Amanullah said: "Anna! Let's wrestle."

One time, in Qaqa Satar's car in Mazar-e-Sharif, Amanullah had turned around in the passenger seat and plunked his hand on my knee. I remembered that hand. It was broad and fleshy. His wrist was as thick as my thigh. He probably could snap my neck with two fingers.

I played the gender card.

"You can't wrestle with me," I said. "I'm a woman."

"But you can wrestle with *me*!" And with a roar, Asad leapt to his feet and pounced upon Amanullah, and the men spun on the ground, kicking up sand and aurum dust and growling and panting and laughing, and now the wind carried their laughter as well.

On the walk back to Oqa, we caught up with some boys who were molesting a Horsfield's tortoise. It was about eight inches long, and it had retreated into its shell of nut-brown scutes that blanched at the edges to a sickly yellow. The boys took turns stepping on it with their rubber-sandaled feet. Then one of the boys kicked it with gusto. A little gratuitous act of sadism, of an innate viciousness each of us carries within. Horsfield's tortoises are native to Afghanistan and live up to one hundred years. How old was this one? Which other depravities, grand and small, had it witnessed? Soon the boys lost interest in the tortoise and followed us into the village, spitting and giggling, holding hands, hopping over thorny shrubs and lumps of dried and drying human excrement and a rusted mortar shell. I looked back and the reptile was gone.

That night I went to bed in my rental room in Mazar-e-Sharif. My scalp was full of sand and maybe—I liked to believe—some gold. The gale outside had become a storm. Half asleep, I imagined dunes marching past Oqa in a macabre and biblical cavalcade. Then I imagined that I would wake up the next morning and see the Hindu Kush upside down, or rearranged into a circle. But no. Nothing external ever budged these cold mountains, neither wind nor blood nor grief, nor even a call to prayer under a smoky sunrise.

When I returned to Oqa, I couldn't tell whether the dunes had shifted at all.

〜〜〜

The village slacked through its forenoons.

After the goats had been dispatched to pasture and the boys had been dispatched to pick kindling and the dough had been kneaded in large blue-glazed ceramic basins and set under old blankets to rise for paltry lunches of nan and tea, a lassitude spilled over Oqa. A hard-earned lethargy that sagged like translucent cling wrap between the sun-bleached wasteland and the faded stratum of the sky.

During these hours, women would drift from house to house to ask for a quarter cup of salt or to gossip. Men would drift from house to house to smoke cigarettes or opium. Oqans of both genders would gather into small congregations and migrate slowly through the village to gather fodder for the next day's yarn, or simply to squat and gaze, unblinking, at the desert. Neighbors would stray into Thawra's loom room to squat on her loom for a few minutes and tie some knots together.

There was Juma Gul, whose name meant "Friday flower," and who was always smiling and chewing gum. She never stayed very long. Her own carpet was stretched beneath a clothesline onto which she had pinned a drawing she had made, with soot on lined paper, of some primeval god, each of its stick arms and legs ending in three long talons. She said it was to explain human anatomy to her youngest daughter, who was three.

Jahan Gul, World Flower, whose house was taken up almost entirely by a twenty-four-foot-long loom so old the gargantuan unfinished carpet upon it had overgrown with goat vertebrae sucked clean, skeins of thread, drying lozenges of donkey dung, blankets.

Choreh Gul, Resolution Flower, gaunt and bird-faced and heavy-lidded with opium, would come by with or without her jovial ten-year-old daughter, Hazar Gul, One Thousand Flowers. These two wove with Thawra often and for the longest stretches, in exchange for a fraction of the proceeds from the carpet. Choreh Gul did not have a loom of her own because her husband, Choreh, couldn't afford the yarn, and because there was no place to put a loom in her single-room house anyway. She had six children in various stages of infirmity. When her family unrolled their flimsy mattresses at night upon the thin bazaar-bought blankets that kept the dust down on the earthen floor, the only space not taken was the small bare square around an old and poorly soldered *bukhari*, which belched more smoke than heat. On a windowsill of their house, the tangled heap of wires that were intended to connect the generator to the power

line, wires the villagers had entrusted Choreh to keep, shone with silver dust like a severed umbilical cord of some imagined better life.

It took a village to weave a carpet. *Thk, thk, thk,* the sickles counted out the long, sluggish mornings of poverty.

Sometimes something uncommon would take place. An event. For example, Qaqa Satar would spread Baba Nazar's Pakistani rug on the ground, and double and triple over his long frame impressively in prayer: that was an event. The villagers would come to watch that. Or I would pull out my sketchbook to draw. For a few turns that was an event, and the villagers would come to watch that, too. They would click their tongues and nod and giggle in appreciation when they recognized in my messy pen drawings a particular rooster, a neighbor's house.

After a while, my sketching ceased to be an event. The rooster and the house were old things the villagers had already seen and would see again every day, *inshallah*. I wasn't telling them anything new.

A few mornings before the vernal equinox, a man from Toqai, a village half a day's walk through the dunes, brought his she-camel to be serviced by Naim's bull. The men drove the camels, first the female, then the male, to the northern edge of the village, where a soot-blackened ellipsis of tandoor ovens trailed off toward the dunes, signaling to the heavens some unformulated or unfinished wish, some hint not taken. By the time the bull had been brought, lolling out a narrow purple tongue and perfuming himself in anticipation with a bristly, urine-soaked tail, all the village men had gathered to squat in a wide circle in fascinated hush. This was as close to porn as it ever got in Oqa.

The animals faced the dunes. She knelt and flared her slanted nostrils, and the narrow veined velvet of her nose trembled. He, delirious, ground his teeth with a pleading high-pitched squeak and dribbled long strings of white foamy saliva libidinously onto the convulsing hump of his mate. For half an hour the entire hummock shuddered with the tremendous throaty grunts of her astonishing desire. Beneath eyelashes long and sparse and hard like cousinia petals, the wide-open dark glassy eyes of the camels reflected the aquamarine sky upon which filamentous cirri gathered and dispersed.

"Once a year only!" Amanullah exclaimed in a deferential whisper. Qaqa Satar snapped a photograph with his cell phone.

On the periphery of that gathering, next to a tandoor lit with dry grass, Choreh Gul and Hazar Gul had come out to bend over a stack of large uncooked sundials of nan and pies stuffed with bitter orach. On her right hand Choreh Gul wore a soiled quilted mitt, and between her teeth she clenched a large nail. She took the nail, pierced each loaf four times so that the bread wouldn't billow from the heat too much, and bit the nail again. One by one, she placed the loaves onto the mitt, slathered them with the opaque well water her daughter had brought in a dinged aluminum basin, then slapped them onto the inside wall of the oven. Tatters of kindling fire ran in the wind and black smoke curled out and drifted over the squatting men and the mating animals. With her unmittened hand, Choreh Gul scooped palmfuls of water and threw them at the cooking loaves. The oven sibilated. A satisfied and benevolent god hissing at a woman and a girl at the edge of the world. Behind them bread-colored dunes rose.

The men who were watching the camels took no interest in this mundane magic. Someone in Oqa was baking bread every day. In thirty minutes, the she-camel's owner, who would get to keep the single calf when it was born after fifteen months of gestation, would take her back to Toqai. The villagers would talk about those thirty minutes for days.

Later that week, the villagers stood next to Baba Nazar's house with their faces upturned. An American B-52 Stratofortress was refueling in the blue blue sky above Oqa.

The bomber rendezvoused with a KC-135 Stratotanker at an altitude of more than five miles somewhere beyond the citadel of ancient Balkh and drifted eastward. The planes at first a palm apart, then a thumb, then a pinkie. Until the bomber slid behind and slightly underneath the tanker. The Oqans could just make out the gossamer refueling boom that extended from the tanker's rear to the unseen receptacle above the B-52's cockpit. For a few minutes, the two silver machines glided together. They banked slightly, they straightened out, all in unison. Locked in an unearthly rendition of the most important of all earthly rituals, absolutely alone above these camel-colored plains.

One tanker could carry thirty-one thousand gallons of fuel—enough to run Oqa's generator to power the village every night for more than fourteen years. One B-52 could carry eighteen two-thousand-pound "smart" bombs, fifty-one five-hundred-pound bombs, almost thirty thousand cluster bomblets, and twelve nuclear cruise missiles. Enough to erase Oqa from the face of the Earth and pulverize the Hindu Kush into a barchan colony, or not even that. The Oqans did not make such calculations. They held their breath and watched and watched, and still they could not decide whether this bizarre, bellicose erotica at twenty-seven thousand feet was proof of the Americans' vulnerability or omnipotence.

In a few minutes, the bomber pulled back and banked north and scythed the ice-blue sky and vanished over Uzbekistan's airspace. Soon the tanker was also gone.

The villagers talked about that for a few days, too.

〜〜〜

One bleak cold morning, on a quest for diversion, a small deputation of men and women crammed into Choreh Gul's threadbare house. She was sitting on her haunches by the *bukhari*, trying to keep warm. Her youngest son, Zakrullah, squirmed next to her on a blanket quilted from old rags.

The neighbors watched Choreh Gul reach inside her dress of blue and white rayon and pull out a pendulous right breast. Barren. No milk at all. Sucked dry by life on this loess ridge that jutted out of a desert just as barren. By days of dividing up pittances of rice for breakfast, lunch, and dinner among her family. By her five other children. You see? Choreh Gul pitched forward and, kneeling now, lifted her deflated breast by a pinch of pale skin. She dangled it like a white flag of defeat. She looked down at it accusingly. As though she hoped to shame it into lactating. Then she tucked it inside the dress again, sat back on her haunches, shrugged.

A pathetic thing, this breast.

The neighbors murmurously agreed.

Zakrullah, for whom this useless breast was intended, writhed soundlessly, naked from the waist down. Forty days old and hungry. Loose and wrinkled and spookily old skin drooped from his angular pelvis. His shirt and two quilt coats tinkled with the coins Choreh Gul had sewn onto his clothes to ward off evil spirits. His scalp and forehead glowed a fluorescent fuchsia from the permanganate solution with which she had slathered his head. She thought maybe it would help with his headaches. She thought maybe he had headaches. And even if he didn't, the permanganate solution and the amulets were the best she could do for Zakrullah. Since she had no milk.

Zakrullah coughed once.

The neighbors nodded at the baby in a kind of unsurprised resignation. They agreed that he, indeed, was quite ill. They agreed that nothing could be done for him: no woman in Oqa had enough milk to spare for someone else's infant, and no one had the time or the means to take him to the free doctor in Dawlatabad. They also agreed that most newborns in Oqa looked like that after a few weeks, and many of them survived.

〜〜〜

L ate-winter wind blew merciless and raw, and drew a gunmetal sheet of clouds over the melancholy plains. Half a dozen dust devils moored the gray land to the gray sky. The wind had brought a biting drizzle like myriad glass shards to Mazar-e-Sharif, bleached the city of color, slathered it with ankle-deep mud. The Hindu Kush floated above low clouds like brushstroke mountains in a Japanese ink miniature.

But in Oqa, not a drop fell. Not even to spot the slate dust, let alone coax new plants out of it, and the village goats had just about denuded whatever forage was left in the threadbare wasteland.

"I don't know," Amanullah had said that morning, screwing up his strabismic eyes. As though his squinting could have squeezed some green out of the cold, sheet-iron plains. "Must be something wrong with us."

Qaqa Satar's Toyota jerked and squeaked over tussocks and ruts in this bleak desert. In the backseat Choreh Gul was carsick. She had never been in a car before. From time to time, Qaqa Satar would stop the car, and she would get out and vomit discreetly, as only a woman in a burqa could. Then she would gather up the wind-whipped and billowing nylon ruches of her veil and climb back into the car and take Zakrullah from her husband's lap, and Qaqa Satar would slowly depress the gas pedal again. Another half a mile conquered. Zakrullah was going to the doctor after all.

Choreh Gul had greeted my idea that Zakrullah should travel to the government hospital in Dawlatabad in Qaqa Satar's car with little enthusiasm. It seemed like a chore. It seemed like a very long journey for just one child—and what to do with the other five, two girls and three boys, while she was away? Also, her husband Choreh would have to come with her because for a woman to travel outside the village without a grown male relative was dangerous and improper even in a burqa, and that would mean that for the day of the drive Choreh would not be able to scavenge the dunes for ancient coins and jewelry that he usually huckstered to middlemen in town. Losing a day of such work could mean losing more than a day of sustenance. Choreh Gul had been dubious the trip to the hospital would be worth all the hassle.

It was additionally possible, though she had not said any such thing out loud, that Choreh Gul also had harbored the common anxiety of an addict: that at the hospital she would not be allowed to take the minuscule nuggets of opium she, like most of Oqa's women, diluted in her morning tea. Opium was much cheaper than rice and it helped stave off hunger and woe. Choreh Gul and her husband spent between two and four dollars a month on the drug. Food—flour for bread, rice and the oil to cook it with, and tea—could cost five times as much.

In any case, in her room reeking of urine, dust, manure, and straw, of the acrid smoke from the *bukhari* and of Choreh's opium pipe, the woman had contemplated the offer that Qaqa Satar drive her and Zakrullah to see a doctor at the free government clinic, and the responsibility that her accepting this offer had entailed, and had responded: "I have to ask my husband."

When her husband had returned from the desert two days later, he said the idea of taking his youngest to see a doctor was just fine. Late the next morning, Qaqa Satar and I delivered the couple and their infant son inside the metal gate of Dawlatabad District Hospital.

Flip-flopped and tentative, Choreh Gul and Choreh shuffled into the unheated pediatric ward. Choreh Gul had pulled back the front flap of her burqa and carried her swaddled child past unoccupied cots that sagged under the hard memory of untold repetitions of ailing weight. Brown smears of old blood or old excrement or both stained the blue-green dado like auxiliary wainscoting from hell.

A German relief agency had built the hospital with concrete several years earlier, and construction workers had skimped on insulation. Maybe there had been none available. The wind leaked cold and damp through cracks in the windowpanes. A doctor and three nurses worked here but only one of that team was present, a stout and stern young nurse named Faruza. Nurse Faruza wore her white doctor's coat as a pro forma afterthought between a floor-length wool skirt and a down jacket, and she had tucked each hand inside the opposite sleeve of her jacket, using the sleeves as a muff. She looked fatigued. She puckered her lipsticked mouth in disdain at the pauperized and bedraggled trinity that had shambled into her domain, then unpuckered it and ordered Choreh Gul to lay her son on a desk draped with a plastic tablecloth and unwrap him. The skeletal and wincing baby emerged into the cold, naked on top of his quilted tatters. The nurse took in the anorexic thighs, the slatboard ribcage, the wrinkled skin wilting on the pelvic bones, nodded, and said: "He's fine."

She did not remove her hands from her jacket sleeves, did not touch the infant. It was too cold. "He does not look malnourished."

Overwhelmed by Nurse Faruza's glacial authority, Choreh Gul and Choreh said nothing and stood still. The nurse mistook their silence for mulishness. She sighed, took her hands out of their sleeve muff, fished a cell phone from the right thigh pocket of her uniform coat, and dialed the doctor.

"He does not have a problem with malnutrition," said Doctor Mohammed Akbar when he arrived a few minutes later wearing jeans and a leather jacket and the battered look of someone resigned to not ameliorating the tragedies of this world.

"My son is very thin. Could you give him some drugs, please?" Choreh said.

The doctor studied very carefully and with great sadness the excreta-smeared wall. Perhaps he expected some help from there. He tried again: "If they are under six months old, we cannot accept them."

But he reached over the desk and over the infant lying upon the desk anyway and opened a drawer and removed a stethoscope from it. He closed his eyes and listened to Zakrullah's chest with his eyes closed. Then he opened his eyes and said: "I suppose we can send him to the lab to check for giardiasis and dysentery."

He turned to Choreh. His eyes welled with accusation.

"Do you give opium to the baby? Don't lie to me, because I will check and see." He folded the stethoscope and put it back in the drawer and for the first time spoke to me. The guileless foreign benefactor who had to be set straight. "It is very common for people in this area to give opium to children when they cry. They are either giving opium to them or he is ingesting it with her milk."

Even so, the doctor was getting worked up. Was it something he heard in Zakrullah's chest? Or in his own—some once-upon-a-time aspiration not yet completely expunged by toil at a shitty district hospital in Northern Afghanistan? He scrutinized Zakrullah now, as though he had never noticed the baby before. The rib bones, the withered face, the slack-skin sacks of thighs. Then he straightened his shoulders and pronounced in a voice suddenly sonorous and grave: "He is deteriorating. The baby must stay at the hospital for three days. His mother must stay with him. She will be fed three meals a day and the baby will be given medicine for free. Ampicillin and gentamicin. He was in danger when you brought him in. We will begin treatment immediately."

Nurse Faruza pointed to a cot, and Choreh Gul wrapped the blankets over her son and slipped out of her plastic sandals and climbed onto the cot and sat there with her legs tucked in. Almost inaudibly, Zakrullah began to cry. His mother reached inside her dress and pulled out her thin left breast and gave him the empty nipple. Emotionless. Slow. A strung-out Madonna in a filthy district hospital. Then she looked up and called: "I also need some drugs."

But the doctor did not hear her request. He was already out the door and shouting out orders for naloxone for a new patient who had just arrived in the grubby anteroom of the pediatric ward. The patient's name was Abdul Bashir. He was fifteen days old and dying of an opium overdose.

~~~~

The next morning it was still overcast. Oyster light sifted through the windows into Thawra's loom room, where in this dull glow she worked the warps and wefts alone in patient silence. Next door, in Amanullah's bedroom, Choreh and a few neighbors, men and boys, had taken shelter from the weather. The boys squatted on the uncarpeted section of the floor by the door, where the dusty rows of the men's shoes and flip-flops attended like antediluvian witnesses in their own right, talced and venerable. Their owners reclined on mattresses and shared an opium pipe and stories of addiction.

The pipe was soldered of sooty iron and shaped like a poppy seedpod on a thick stem, and belonged to Amin Bai, the Commander. He had dispatched Amanullah's seven-year-old son, Nurullah, to fetch it from his house. The opium was Amin Bai's also, a brown-black disk weighing about a fifth of an ounce that he kept wrapped in a folded sheet of lined paper ripped out of some notebook and tucked into the chest pocket of his *shalwar kameez*. A quarter-size gobbet and in Oqa worth probably a quarter of a dollar. Not thirty miles to the northeast, men more adventurous than the Commander carried the precious narcotic resin across the Amu Darya to Uzbekistan, where it was worth hundreds of times more. The previous year their cargo had amounted to ninety metric tons—approximately four hundred and fifty million disks such as the one Amin Bai kept in his pocket—and, together with the three hundred tons of the drug smuggled out of Afghanistan through Iran and Pakistan, supplied nearly all of the world's opium. At four billion dollars a year, opium trade in Afghanistan was the second-largest source of revenue after international aid and made up approximately half the budget of the Taliban. Baba Nazar knew a couple of men from Toqai who had carried opium to Uzbekistan and returned rich. He also knew a couple of men from Toqai who had carried opium to Uzbekistan and were shot crossing the border.

"And sent back," he said, and punctuated the smoky air with a gnarled forefinger. "Their dead bodies."

Amin Bai, Choreh, and Qaqa Satar took turns heating the resin over a low conical oil lamp, which they had set in the center of the *namad*-covered floor. Prostrate mendicants before a fickle deity that enslaved and granted analgesia both. Opium smoke filled the room quickly and pearled by the low windows beyond which an indifferent and ageless desert sheened under a flat gray sky. Halfway to the ceiling the vapor, chilled, smoothed out into a pale and opaque film. It smelled slightly sour, like burning yeast.

Afghanistan's opium habit was more than two thousand years old, introduced, it is believed, by Alexander the Great, whose troops had used it as a palliative. Dating individual addiction was trickier. Amin Bai could not remember the first time he had tasted opium, probably because he had been an infant then. Choreh, who was forty-one, said he had started smoking in his early thirties, after a land-mine incident. He had ventured a hundred yards or so into the sand dunes to collect some calligonum kindling in order to boil water for tea and had been chopping at a tough, gnarled stem with a pick when the pick struck a mine. He supposed the Soviets had placed the mine when their soldiers had been stationed at a barracks on the north side of the dunes in the 1980s. The shrapnel had torn a palm-size chunk of flesh out of his right thigh and lacerated his calf with a web of zigzagging and vermiform scars and strange runic indentations that still chafed against the trouser leg of his brown *shalwar kameez*. He said opium helped dull the pain. He also said his wife had started taking opium just before she became pregnant with Zakrullah, to stop the aches in her legs and neck and shoulders.

"But after the New Year, I will join the police," Choreh announced. "They offer a good salary, ten thousand afghanis. And they also have a program to treat opium addiction."

Choreh's neighbors shifted on their mattresses and coughed in scoffing protest at this version of history. They said Choreh Gul had been drinking opium at least since Choreh had brought her to Oqa from Khairabad as a fifteen-year-old bride, and that had been more than twenty years back. They also said Choreh himself had been smoking since his teens. Boys in Oqa were allowed to start smoking opium when they turned fifteen, or when they got married, whichever came first.

As for his New Year's resolution, it was as good as any they'd ever heard, and they had heard them many times, from many men in Oqa, for Oqa was a village of dreamers.

Choreh shrugged, slowly, groggily. What was it to them? They and their own wives were smoking and drinking opium, too. He didn't see any of them quitting or joining the police, either.

At that the men nodded with the solemn approval they granted any truth, no matter how disagreeable. Almost everyone in Oqa was using opium, they said, that was true—except for the children who weren't sick. Children seemed to be sick all the time.

Amin Bai stoked up the oil lamp again, and Qaqa Satar checked the pipe, inhaled with his eyes skewed, and sang out: "It's very nice. It's very sweet. If you smoke it and you want to have sex with your wife, you'll go for a whole hour. It makes your whole body feel warm. You feel like you are in a garden in London. Women who weave add a tiny bit to a cup of tea and it allows them to work long hours. They don't feel muscle cramps, no pain."

"If you have a cough and you smoke it, the cough is gone," Baba Nazar chimed in. He himself did not smoke because—opium's medicinal properties aside—he believed it was unhealthy. "I have smoked only once, and I threw up. It is very strong. If you eat a small amount, you'll be dizzy for twenty-four hours. I'm seventy, and I can walk and work. I'm stronger than these people"—he swept his arm toward his guests—"because I don't use it."

Once upon a time, Baba Nazar had been a champion wrestler in Oqa, Karaghuzhlah, and Khairabad, a crown he still gloated about, and he took his health seriously.

Amanullah didn't smoke because his father had forbidden it.

Instead, he squatted by the door amid the shoes and the children, and busied himself with replacing a piece of rabbit skin on Baba Nazar's *tupcha* with a fresher one. Nurullah and some older boys knelt quietly at his elbows, reverential, silent. Their eyes darted between Amanullah's handiwork and the men who were passing the pipe back and forth. All of them had tasted opium. In a few years they would be old enough to smoke it, too.

The men listened carefully to the story of the infant Abdul Bashir.

The baby had thrashed against the soiled Dawlatabad hospital cot and gurgled the deep, horrible, rhythmic wheezes of the dying. He had begun to convulse when the nurses had pressed his tiny face, blue from asphyxiation, into an adult oxygen mask larger than his head. They tourniqueted his spasming limbs one by one to find a threadlike vein that could fit a needle so that they could resuscitate him with a milliliter of the opiate blocker naloxone, and seconds dragged like hours until the antidote kicked in and the baby cried at last.

Doctor Akbar, the pediatrician, said that every single one of the approximately one thousand child patients his hospital received each year, Choreh's son Zakrullah included, had some degree of opium poisoning when they arrived, even if they had been brought in to be treated for other ailments—meningitis, say, or cholera. He said also that each year a handful were brought to the hospital already dead from overdose. But for a few minutes' delay Abdul Bashir would have been one of those.

Abdul Bashir's statuesque and stunning mother fixed her child with a drugged stare. Twenty-four years old, fair-skinned, and lissome in her white sheepskin coat, her high cheekbones flushed from running from the outskirts of Dawlatabad with the baby in her arms, wringing her long, silver-ringed and hennaed fingers: a would-be infanticidal pietà who herself had been born addicted. It was she who had given Abdul Bashir the opium that morning, to hush his crying, but she must have miscalculated the dose. After he stopped breathing, she brought him to the hospital.

At this part of the story, Baba Nazar laughed and the rest of the men in his house laughed as well.

Why? Could this not have happened with one of their own babies, here in Oqa?

"No-ho-ho," the Commander said, coughing as he guffawed. "Here, we know the trick, how much opium to give a baby."

The men chuckled some more at the young mother's incompetence, and Nurullah and the other boys grinned, happy for the occasion to express their camaraderie with important grown men of such expertise. Outside, the wind had died down. The desert swelled with the enormous silences of a carpet-shaped world that was chockfull of vital mistakes and whose pain threshold was limitless.

〰〰〰

A flotilla of perfectly round and cartoonish clouds sailed over my walled compound in Mazar-e-Sharif. It was the morning of the vernal equinox, the first morning of spring and, according to

the Zoroastrian calendar by which Afghanistan fixed its time, the morning of Nawruz: New Year's Day. That year, the holiday fell on a Tuesday.

"*Sal-e-Nau mubarak!*" Happy New Year! Men leaned out past heavy gates of red and turquoise sheetmetal, cranking them open just a tad wider than usual to usher in a little extra of the year's first sunshine. The holiday's name, Nawruz, meant "new day," or "new light," in Farsi.

"*Wa shoma ham Sal-e-Nau mubarak.*" And a happy New Year to you, as well. Women greeted early guests with *haft mewa*, a heady compote of dried fruit and nuts drowned in giant vats of boiling water and steeped overnight, and *samanak*, a sweet paste of wheat germ, sugar, and walnuts. Only women were allowed to prepare *samanak*, and a few days before the holiday they had taken turns stirring it for twenty-four hours over wood fires in their walled yards and singing and trading vulgar jokes and braiding one another's hair and trying on one another's lipstick. Traditionally, had a man glimpsed the preparation, the dessert would have had to be thrown out, and the man derided.

A twelve-year-old boy in my house inscribed on graph paper the nascent year's name: 1390, per a countdown formally begun in the last decade of the Sassanid rule of the Khorasan. The holiday itself was so old its origins were lost. As old as man's Manichaean desire to simplify the world into manageable opposites, light and dark, good and evil.

On city roundabouts, papier-mâché tulips bloomed. At the Blue Mosque, Zoroaster's reputed burial place, thousands of white doves cooed in satiated unison, and mullahs prepared to welcome pilgrims descending upon the city from all over Central Asia. This was Mazar-e-Sharif, the city of mystics, and both the mullahs and the visitors were eager to forsake Islam for a day of pre-Mohammedan hedonism that culminated with the raising of a ribboned and beaded maypole in the mosque's vast yard tiled with black-and-white marble. For a week already, hunched dervishes from Iran in swags of rosaries had been pounding sidewalk dust with their walking staffs, entranced, declaiming fervently and at random to passing cars and horse-drawn buggies and motorcycles snippets of decadent verse by Omar Khayyam and Hafez, and drawing stares. Domestic and international politicians and luminaries were also expected. Ten thousand policemen and soldiers in armored vests blotted the sun-gorged streets because city officials anticipated a major terrorist act. The terrorist act would rend the city ten days later, when six Taliban

75

would lead an enraged Friday mob from the Blue Mosque to the United Nations offices to topple guard towers, set walls ablaze, and, beneath the alluvial slopes bloodred with wild spring poppies, slaughter twelve of the agency's employees, mostly Westerners. On Nawruz, though, war seemed to be elsewhere—on the other side of the Hindu Kush, where most of the hundred and forty thousand foreign troops and elusive and sandaled guerrillas were fighting one another and killing and maiming in the process farmers and day laborers and their families with roadside bombs and missiles and small artillery, or at the very least outside the city limits, where insurgency was quietly gathering steam, uncontested, unstoppable.

The day passed in comings and goings of guests, in exchanges of kisses and the euphonious singsong of greetings. The family in whose house I was renting a room did not go to the Blue Mosque to watch the maypole ceremony—too dangerous, they said, not worth the risk. Instead, they celebrated the New Year indulging in the discreet domestic pleasures of Afghanistan's wannabe bourgeoisie, taking in the sun and telling jokes and smoking a mint-flavored waterpipe on a *takht*, a carpeted and pillowed wooden platform they had established in the center of the yard. Guests and family members of both genders and all ages took turns shaking off their slippers and climbing on, dragging on the pipe, sipping tea and *haft mewa* from glass cups, shucking sunflower seeds into cupped palms, squinting at the tall sky, moving around the dial of the *takht* to make room for newcomers, and talking, talking. Like guests at the Mad Hatter's tea party. Reluctant men peeled off to attend the one-o'clock prayer at the neighborhood mosque, returned an hour later singing folk songs about love, and climbed back upon the *takht* to resume their pagan reverie. The afternoon sun was gentle and flocks of white doves looped, delirious with spring, in air the color of tea. My hosts' children brought out some colored modeling clay and one of the men, a driver who worked for the United Nations, asked me to make something. I made a green cat. He took it in his hand, studied it for a few beats, then very deftly attached three black stripes to it: one around the cat's neck, two across its face.

"That's a collar," I pointed. "What are these?"

"Burqa. This is Afghanistan. Next time don't make without burqa."

No bombs went off in the city that day. There was no gunfire. By six o'clock the first sun of spring softly relayed toward the western hemisphere, and in the caramel evening haze the crest of the Hindu Kush faded into a velvety saffron carpet fringe. Then night erased the mountains altogether and summoned pale stars out of the dark. When the waning moon rose over the eastern stucco wall of the compound, I brought out Peter Hopkirk's *The Great Game* to read by moonlight.

A hundred and seventy-nine years ago and less than twenty miles away, by moonlight also, the Great Game player and British political agent in Kabul Sir Alexander Burnes had found Moorcroft's grave, "unmarked and half covered by a mud wall, outside the town of Balkh." Moorcroft, the veterinary surgeon–explorer in the employ of the East India Company, the first Englishman to set foot on the banks of the Oxus, the man who had warned of Russia's wish to occupy Afghanistan and who had urged Britain to annex it first, was believed to have succumbed to fever in romantic pursuit of the golden Akhal-Tekes, the fabled Turkoman horses.

"Moorcroft," wrote Hopkirk, "thus lies not far from the spot where, more than a century and a half later, Soviet troops and armour poured southwards across the River Oxus into Afghanistan." And now the soldiers of yet another empire were warring upon this land. Some of them were scanning my neighborhood that night from two invisible helicopter gunships that whirred low over the low cityscape to the north of the compound, disrupting the peace or keeping it, or both.

A little blond girl had dozed off on a pillow next to mine. Her name was Avesta, like the mostly lost collection of Zoroastrianism's sacred texts. Her mouth was sticky with *samanak*, and her eyelids glittered with the blue eye shadow her mother had allowed her to wear on New Year's Day. With utmost tenderness, her father scooped her up and carried her to her own thin mattress in the house. Tomorrow would dawn over her eternal war zone a little sunnier, a little warmer.

～～～

As if on cue, the next day the desert spilled a brilliant green. The almond orchards where dreamy flowers just recently had spumed were suddenly powdery green with minuscule teardrop nuts. Goats everywhere kidded all at once. In the pale light before sunup, the sulfuric and deserted wastelands of winter outside Mazar had come instantaneously and noisily to jubilant life: thousands of downy black and spotted kids scuttled, clanging, across fields that at last promised some kind of a harvest. There still had been no rain near Oqa, but here, too, strange sheeny succulents had sprouted through tough unirrigated soil, like some aberrant greenery from outer space.

It was very early and still cold. On the southeastern horizon a yet invisible sun had whitened the narrowest strip of sky, and against it the crest of the Hindu Kush had begun to silhouette grand and black. To the still dark northeast, on the border with Uzbekistan, the lights of Khairatan diffracted from beyond the Earth's curvature, turning the grimy border port into a grandiose city of shimmering skyscrapers. A mirage behooving a historical landmark: in 1989 the last Soviet soldiers had marched across Khairatan's Friendship Bridge and out of Afghanistan after a decade of occupation, leaving behind more than one million dead Afghans and Russians, ten million land mines, and an intractable internecine war that bled into all the wars that came before and after. Then again, everywhere in the Khorasan there were such landmarks. Some glowed, like Khairatan. Others seemed to absorb all light around them. Most just were. Which vanquished army had made its last stand on the land now buried under Oqa's dunes? Whose oblique former castle a half-hour walk west from the village had eroded into a mound of clay? Amanullah told me it was very old. How old? "It was built in 3890," he said.

What difference did a date make? "Time costs nothing in these parts," the Swiss journalist Annemarie Schwarzenbach wrote of the Afghan plains many wars ago, in the 1930s. Dates were just a patina on an overeducated brain. There was no Nawruz celebration in Oqa, no *samanak* parties, no compote of dried fruit to offer guests. The only time that mattered in the village was the tempo of the planet's dual revolutions, the eternal repetition that brought the changing of the seasons, the night and the day, and the magical twilight in between.

Twilight in Oqa. The stars extinguished one by one, leaving Venus to greet the sun alone. In the spectral predawn blue on the western edge of the village, Amanullah, Boston, and Baba Nazar were running jackknifed at the waist with outstretched arms in a farcical bourrée after a black-and-white scatter of day-old kid goats. The kids had to be gathered up and stuffed into one of Baba Nazar's shacks so that Shareh and Hafez, the village herders, could take the family's half-dozen nannies to distant pasture without the newborns following. The dusky hollow south of the hummock stirred with the goatherds' short whoops and the bells and musty bleating of a herd already on its way to the desert. The boy Hafez, named with the honorific reserved for someone who has memorized the Koran, the book this unschooled child will never read. Named also after the fourteenth-century Sufi poet whose verses Afghan men recited apothegmatically, unprompted. Hafez the goatherd, bowlegged and weatherworn from having spent his whole short life in relentless dry wind and flinty sun. Whose beauty fanned his secret ecstasies? Which lonesome ghazals did he compose to the scattershot tinkling of his flock as his heart swelled with spring?

Boston threw the last kid into the shed, drew a large wooden latch over the door of unevenly nailed boards, pressed her back against it in mock exhaustion, and stood there giggling. A goldpink cloud spilled in the east where the sun would soon crown, and in that glow the wrinkles on Boston's face rearranged themselves, and for a second on that morning in late March this old woman was a little girl who had just had the luck of sinking her fingers into the silken fleece of newborn goats.

Work finished for now, Boston and the men sauntered back to the main house, and Amanullah lit the *bukhari* in one of the rooms. The dry grass took to flame at once, and Boston balanced on the stove a blackened pitcher with water to boil for tea. Amanullah plopped onto a mattress and assumed his favorite position, horizontal. Lying down could mean falling asleep, and sleep sometimes brought Amanullah dreams vivid and almost as wonderful as the forbidden journeys he would never take.

"Sometimes I have dreams so good they make me happy for several days. Even for a month!" The mere memories of these dreams transported him to some other spring. "For example, if I dream of a young girl, maybe twenty years old, who comes up to me and hugs me and kisses me—that can make me happy for a long time."

Baba Nazar unstoppered the plastic-wrapped cork of his old Chinese thermos, poured hot stove-boiled water over a handful of green tea leaves, replaced the cork, and set the tea to brew for a spell. He unfolded on the floor a *dastarkhan* of white and lavender houndstooth plastic in which his wife had wrapped a hardening loaf of yesterday's nan. He unstoppered the thermos again and poured the tea. It was time for breakfast, and stories.

"There are seven stars," Baba Nazar said. He crumbled the tough bread into his tea and sucked at the rim of the glass cup.

"Four brothers and three sisters. Brothers in the front and sisters in the back. Their parents are dead, and when these stars die, they will see their parents in paradise.

"But some say," he continued, "the three stars are children, and the four stars are the bed on which the children are carrying their dead parents."

The Pleiades, a constellation of orphans four hundred light-years away. Somehow Baba Nazar's story seemed sadder than the Greek myth of seven distraught sister-nymphs who had plunged to their deaths, then ascended to the sky to shine. Perhaps because in Oqa death always seemed just a breath away. Thawra flitted past the door, taciturn and sequined like an echo of a shooting star, and disappeared into the loom room. *Thk, thk, thk.* Baba Nazar crumbled some more bread in time with the subtle pulse of the weaver's sickle.

What about dragons, the stylized, angular dragons that sometimes slinked along the borders of Oqa's carpets? The old man could not think of any, though I have been told, by a young Hazara taxi driver from Karaghuzhlah, that until just two years earlier, a big monster dragon had lived in a fallow field south of his village.

"It was like a snake, but it would sometimes turn into something bigger, like a lizard," said the driver, whose name was Qasim. "Then it disappeared. For forty years people couldn't cross the field. It probably died, because people said the field smelled funny two years ago." Qasim had never seen the monster, nor did he know anyone who had. But his grandfather and uncles had told him it had been there.

Once, not far from Oqa's cemetery, I saw a desert monitor lizard turn its five-foot-long Mesozoic body slowly in the dust.

What about nomad warriors, then, I asked Baba Nazar—the ancient horsemen of the Pazyryk? The belligerence of the Turkomans once had been the stuff of the legends that nurtured the Europeans' image of an Afghanistan entrenched, implacable, hostile. Descendants of an orphan and a she-wolf, inventors of the stirrupped saddle, who had written in runes and buried their horses with their men. Francis Skrine and Edward Denison Ross, in their 1899 tome *The Heart of Asia*, had called the Turkomans "a race with whom no peace or truce was possible," "untamed tribes" who possessed "some at least of the traits of the noble savage of fiction." "'He who puts his hand to his sword-hilt,'" the Englishmen cited a Turkoman proverb, "'hath no need to ask for a good reason.'"

But the only transient Turkomans of whom Baba Nazar knew were the families who had fled the Soviet annexation of Central Asia in the 1920s. Hundreds of thousands of refugees had poured into Bactria then, across the desert from the newly created Turkestan Autonomous Soviet Socialist Republic, and across the Amu Darya from Soviet Uzbekistan and Tajikistan. "A lot of them were our ancestors," the hunter said. "I probably have some distant cousins and aunts in Turkmenistan. Or maybe in Uzbekistan. If I go on Uzbek television and say that I have an ancestor from Uzbekistan, and the Uzbek government finds the rest of my family, then we can move to Uzbekistan. One family in Khairabad went to Uzbekistan that way."

A hereditary wanderlust stirred in the hunter, a yearning half-forgotten and now loosened in the way spring loosens pent-up aches.

"Life in Uzbekistan is very good," Baba Nazar daydreamed. He had not heard of the poverty on the other side of the border, of prison torture, of villages and towns emptied of men gone to Russia to endure apartheid-style discrimination and beatings in return for menial jobs. "Some people who go there with a visa return. They even cry when the visa expires and they have to come back to Afghanistan."

On his mattress, Amanullah held his breath and hung on to every word. Secretly mapping out another possible escape route, smitten already by the lithe and unveiled beauties he would find on the other side of the river. But only the carpets Thawra wove next door would ever travel from this house beyond the familiar boundaries of Balkh. The men's itinerant fantasies will be that subtle twang that tickles the soles of the carpets' future owners when they step onto the pile in their bare feet.

The *bukhari* had gone out. The men finished their tea, thanked God for breakfast into their upturned palms—*"Bismillah, bismillah"*—and went outside, where the desert now shone with daylight and the blown-glass sky was translucent and white.

~~~

Many years ago at an abandoned Soviet barracks in the dunes, Baba Nazar had pilfered an old iron spring bed and brought it home on a camel. It was the only bed in Oqa. It wintered in the bedroom Baba Nazar and Boston shared, under the shotgun and beside the niche where the hunter kept his binoculars. On winter afternoons Boston would sit on it spraddle-thighed and stretch skeins of yarn over her knees and roll them into balls.

In warm months the hunter and his son would drag the bed into the sun and anchor its uneven and hollow rusted legs on three clay bricks. Then the bed would become the village centerpiece, the Oqa equivalent of a town square, or of a mosque. Men would lounge on it as they would on a *takht* and talk. They would gather around it to listen to newscasts on Baba Nazar's thirty-year-old transistor radio and discuss dispatches from the world beyond their desert, even beyond the serrated Hindu Kush and the Amu Darya. Children would hide under it, run around it in circles chasing one another, and, when Baba Nazar was not looking and when no adults were sitting on it, bounce on the squeaky springs.

This year, Baba Nazar and Amanullah carried the bed outside just before eight in the morning on the second day of the vernal equinox, after breakfast. They established it near the southeastern corner of Thawra's loom room, near the dark hieroglyphs of drying urine that wormed in the dust where the night before someone had been too lazy or too rushed to make it to the dunes. Having determined that the bed would not wobble, Amanullah threw a plaid blanket and a hard cushion over the springs, slipped out of his flip-flops, lay down on the bed on his back so that the front loop of his green-gray turban visored the sun from his eyes, pulled a cell phone out of his shirt pocket, and proceeded to call his friends in Khairabad. The cell-phone transmitter on the Karaghuzhlah tower worked well that day, and reception was decent.

Villagers began to assemble almost immediately.

First Hazar Gul scurried out of her parents' house grinning, with Zakrullah in her arms, and squatted in the dirt at the foot of the

bed. The infant seemed less pale after three days at the hospital, though it was hard to tell because his mother had swaddled him in several tick blankets and smothered kohl over his eyebrows, eyelids, and forehead, to help Doctor Akbar's treatment stick. Choreh Gul herself emerged slowly into the sun soon after. Her eyes were filmed over, pupils infinitesimally small. She had just taken her morning opium.

Then old Sayed Nafas ambled along and sat down cross-legged on the ground a little apart from Hazar Gul to luxuriate in the warm sun and play with some goat turds. He rolled the turds between the palms of his hands like lozenges or prayer beads, molded them with his fingers. It was a peaceful thing to do on such a fine spring morning, and Sayed Nafas was smiling.

I squatted in the dust and sketched. My doodles no longer attracted the whispering cluster of Oqa's children, the scrutiny of adults, the way Thawra's weaving no longer drew a crowd of boys, for they, like boys everywhere, were only interested in watching the beginning of something new. I sketched a woman I could not recognize for the quivering distance between us hauling water from the southern well. An oblique wall of Baba Nazar's house. A sashless window stuffed with a rolled-up mattress. A chicken. Drawing felt good. It felt as though I, too, was doing something in Oqa rather than observing it; as though, while I was doing it, I belonged. Choreh came stoned and slow, and stood looking at the bed awhile. Deciding whether he should ask to lie on the narrow springs next to Amanullah, or maybe simply feeling the opium caress his body. Then he remembered something. He turned to me and said:

"Buy me a cell phone."

"Sure." I was sketching a camel, unsuccessfully. "If you give me money for it, I'll buy it next time I'm in the city."

"If I had the money, I'd have bought it myself."

Even Hazar Gul laughed at her father's joke.

In the packed clay sloping southward from the bed, Nurullah and a handful of other boys were trying to hit a concrete pylon that stuck out of the sand with pebbles from a distance decided upon by the older boys. A toddler naked from the waist down ran loopy circles, driving before him through the dust a white metal jar cap riveted to the end of a wooden stick with a single nail: a push toy, perhaps the oldest toy in the world, in this oldest place. Two teenagers took turns at an electric pole with slingshots, and the air vibrated with the loud ding of stone on aluminum.

A little after eight Thawra came out of the house carrying Baba

Nazar's transistor radio, put it on the ground by the bed on which her husband was still sprawled out, and turned the dial to a Turkoman channel playing desert music. The rhythm of camel hooves falling on parched earth. Then she returned to the house and soon brought out a green ceramic basin, a green plastic ewer, some faded washrags, and an unlabeled bottle of shampoo. Spring was for spring cleaning.

"Nurullah, come!"

Thawra managed to get the boy to strip off the shirt of his *shalwar kameez*, but the pantaloons he would not take off because only small boys went bare-assed and he was already seven, so she washed him piecemeal over the enamel washbasin. She clasped his scalp with her long fingers and turned it this way and that like a gourd and soaped his short thick black hair and his torso and scoured his ears with a rag. A timeworn ritual. When I was seven, my grandmother used to wash me this way, over a dinged aluminum basin on the creaky and stained kitchen floor of our summer cottage outside Leningrad; it, too, had no plumbing. The morning smelled sweetly of straw, manure, sun, and dust where suds had landed on the ground and were evaporating. Then Boston appeared in the doorway with a broom and proceeded to sweep out the house onto all of this: the young woman, the washbasin, the old towels on the packed clay, the white lather over the boy's brown naked back shivering and covered with goose bumps, Amanullah chattering away on his cheap prepaid phone. Thawra shook her head but said nothing. All daughters-in-law endure such insidious undoings.

Thawra was soaping Nurullah for the second time when Hazar

Gul jumped up, shifted Zakrullah from one arm to the other, and pointed at the sky.

"*Trrna!*" she cried. "*Trrna, trrna!*"

Thawra stood up, white to her elbows with suds and smiling, and Nurullah, free of her grip at last, foam sliding down his back and under the rope belt of his pantaloons, jumped up to see. Amanullah rose from the bed so fast all the springs creaked at once like an accordion dropped open. Boston wheeled around, holding on to her broom, and Baba Nazar hurried out of the house clutching his binoculars. Sayed Nafas released the goat turds and helped himself up from the ground with both hands. Even Choreh Gul got up, swaying and vague. Soon the whole village, it seemed, was outside and calling at the sky: *Trrna! Trrna! Trrna!*

And the sky—viscous like glycerin, crystalline over the white-washed plains, so bright at its apex you could barely discern the sun in the center of that superb irradiance—the slow sky of March quivered with the thinnest ash-blue vein of wings and called back with a song that was fifty million years old.

Trrna!

〰〰

Cranes.

Omens of everything. Symbols of eternal life and emissaries of death. Whimsical, ephemeral, imperiled, and immortal, the oldest birds on the planet. The only large birds that can wing through indigo nights and over cold water, unfettered to diurnal oscillations

of thermals—or soar up, up, up on a current of warm air until they are more than four miles above ground, beyond clouds, beyond sight, in heaven, vanished. Exquisite dancers that have danced into creation myths on five continents. Whose valiant fidelity and Paleocene song have inspired the grandiose Indian epic *Ramayana* and the quietude of the haiku master Bashō. "The mystic crane," Rumi, Balkh's own most famous mystic, called them. The day after Nawruz, fulfilling an annual promise, a sedge of demoiselle cranes en route from a winter in India to their breeding grounds in the Caspian steppes glided down to rune with their cuneiform tracks the parched dunes west of Oqa.

Where Baba Nazar the hunter had been expecting them.

The previous afternoon the old man had spied a handful of crane scouts carve through the sky and descend over a patch of desert where the southernmost barchans licked at the hard-packed clay, the same spot the cranes had picked as a resting spot year after year, migration after migration, millennium after millennium. Demoiselles travel in flocks of up to four hundred, but a few birds usually fly ahead to guide the others to the resting ground. The hunter knew this. He had put on his glasses with the missing bow, adjusted the string that affixed them to his head, unfolded an old burlap sack, poured into it some coarsely milled wheat, mixed in the strychnine he had kept for the occasion, and gone on a short and purposeful hike.

When Hazar Gul spotted the cranes over Oqa the next day, Baba Nazar dispatched his son to the dunes.

An hour later Amanullah revved his scooter up the hummock. Nurullah rode pillion. Dust roiled as if the riders had just broken out of purgatory. Boston's handmade saddlebag hung from the luggage rack behind Nurullah. In each pannier of that saddlebag sat a demoiselle crane.

Baba Nazar lifted the birds out of the bag by their wings one by one and lowered them on the ground. Two heartrending watercolor brushstrokes of the bluest gray that dimmed to penumbral primaries and tail quills. Two fluid question marks of stark black necks. From behind their eyes—red and small like the tart aphrodisiacal berries of the rowan tree—tufted long plumes so unbelievably white it seemed some flame from heaven had licked them there during their flight.

"*Trrna*, baba," Nurullah bragged to his grandfather. The birds' onomatopoeic name an echo of their trumpeting call. But not the call of these two cranes. These uttered rusty croaks like heart valves rupturing, the horrible rasps and wheezes of the opiated infant at the Dawlatabad hospital. They, too, had been poisoned by men.

The cranes could not stand. They crumpled upon the dust. Their wings drooped. One began to convulse, then both. They had stopped croaking and opened their beaks soundlessly now, dripping slime. Their red eyes stuporous, with tiny pupils. Suddenly, one of the birds hissed and struggled halfway up and, gagging, walked several feet backward on the black-iron nodules of its knees and its wings' dark trailing edges. An unholy travesty of a crane dance, a precursor of some devastation yet unknown, a portent of some unutterable trespass.

Then the bird fell, wings spread wide, ataxic, and made no noise again.

"*Trrna!*" called the sky.

A long undulating vee sliced the pale blue tile overhead. Was it a call for the two spread-eagled birds to rise and join the formation? Was it a wail of indignation, of sorrow? A farewell? The poisoned cousins on the ground did not stir. Not yet dead but deadened by the grotesque violence committed against them. Like so many upon the warped loom of this land. Like the dozen women and men and children who had gathered now in a tight circle to gape at this spectacle—the people who wove the most beautiful carpets in the world and now were waiting to see if the poisoned cranes would live or die. And why not? Each winter these villagers put a son, a daughter, a grandchild in the ground not far from the birds' resting spot. ("I ask you, cranes, to warm my child in your wings," an eighth-century Japanese song went.) Perhaps they possessed some terrible knowledge: that one kind of beauty demanded the sacrifice of another. Perhaps they were protecting the very inner chambers of their hearts.

"I heard on the radio once that some unknown disease is killing birds and that they fall out of the sky and die within a day," Baba Nazar said. Smug. Satisfied. "These people on the radio, they didn't know the reason why. And I thought: I do. The reason is my rat poison!"

He had come up with the strychnine trick himself. His father used to sling cranes out of the sky.

Then he turned to Amanullah and said: "There's got to be more out there. Go back and see."

And handed him the shotgun.

Amanullah returned with four more cranes in the saddlebag. One was dead. It had ingested too much strychnine and had been shuddering almost constantly out there in the dunes. Islamic law proscribed eating animals killed by poison, and to keep the bird halal, Amanullah had shot it through the neck. He gave it to his father and laid the other three on the ground.

Five live cranes now lay in the village dirt almost motionless, no longer shaking, their wings flung open, feathers fanned out upon goat droppings and hardening greenish-white splotches of chicken shit, dark blots of dried urine, particles of hay. Amanullah watched the cranes closely lest they, too, began to die and needed to be butchered. It was preferable that they survived: merchants in Mazar paid twelve dollars per bird for live cranes, which they sold to wealthy families to keep as pets. Amanullah kept the phone numbers of a couple of these merchants saved in the memory of his cell phone. Five cranes would sell for almost a third as much as the carpet Thawra was weaving—although at that particular moment she had to interrupt her work again, because Baba Nazar had leaned into the loom room through the gap left by the missing roof and told the woman to spoon into the cranes' bills a mixture of sugar and oil, to force the birds to vomit the poison.

Then he tied the dead crane by the head to the wooden hitching post near Boston's kitchen, reached into the bullet hole in the crane's long and silky neck with his right index finger, and ripped through the skin and feathers, and slipped them off the neck from the hole down, the skin and feathers all at once. With a butchering knife, he severed the wide and hollow trachea that had shaped the crane's immemorial song and smashed off with a hatchet the ulnae and the radii and the tibiotarsi and then slid the skin with its silver-blue plumage off the upper wings and chest and back and thighs. It fell to the ground like a bloodied pearly gown. Boston poured hot tea from an aluminum teapot over the exposed pectorals, granular and dark, stringy with the millions of wingbeats every one of which had carried this crane to its slaughter. Then Baba Nazar untied the dressed bird from the hitching post and laid it on a piece of burlap.

With the hatchet, the old man chopped the breastplate in two, then chopped off the neck halfway up, then turned the bird around and split the back along the spine. He handed the entrails to Boston, splashed some hot tea into the chest cavity, put the dressed meat into a plastic bag, and handed it to Qaqa Satar. That night in Mazar-e-Sharif, the driver's wife will turn it into stew and serve it for dinner. But the strychnine already had contaminated the meat, and everyone in Qaqa Satar's house will cramp from a violent stomachache.

Then Baba Nazar walked over to where the five birds lay prostrate in the dirt, scooped up one—flaccid and disoriented with humiliation and poison—and thrust it at me.

"Take one!"

A year earlier, another Afghan man had offered me a bird, an old man in a soiled turban on a grimy sidewalk in Mazar-e-Sharif. In his hands he had been cupping a white pigeon.

"Take her," the man had said, and lifted the bird for me to see better the wonder he had held captive. The pigeon had fluttered her hollow-boned wings whitely, then settled into his palm again. "Take her."

I had touched the pigeon's neck with my fingertips. "The lunatic clutching a pigeon, stroking it hour after hour / until his fingers and its feathers fuse into a single crumb of tenderness," Julio Cortázar wrote. The caress had enchanted. I could have gone on and on, my skin against her feathers. Soft, weightless. Divine. When she had unfolded her wings again, I could see the marble of her underbelly. And something else. Something awry. I'd looked again. Her legs had been broken.

Before the next morning, one more crane will die. Two will go to a merchant from Mazar-e-Sharif, who will come to pick them up in a *zaranj* motor-rickshaw. Baba Nazar will give them to the merchant for free: "He is a friend," the old man will explain. In Mazar their wings will be clipped, and they will appear for a few months among the painted life-size replicas of deer and duck decoys and live sheep and geese in a gaudy petting-zoo-cum-sculpture in the middle of a rotary on the main road to the airport. The remaining two Baba Nazar will give, also for free, to Amin Bai. The Commander, in turn, will present them as gifts to an old friend of his in Karaghuzhlah, a minor warlord named Hassan Khan, the father of Qasim the taxi driver. For a few nights later in the year Hassan Khan will be my host. I will see the cranes again in his backyard, and something inside me will shrink.

The bored crowd of birdwatchers was thinning. The men left first. Thawra returned to her carpet. A few children hung around to pick up the cranes' limp wings and let them drop again on the ground. The feathers gathered and unfolded like slats on a Japanese hand fan. On a relatively dung-free mound of hardened clay near her house, Choreh Gul had settled, baby Zakrullah in her arms, to watch the cranes through the legs of Amanullah's donkey picketed to a rusted artillery shell casing. Mullahs' prayers were sewn into the bits of cloth on Zakrullah's hat, coins on his blankets jingled for protection from the jinn. Did they work? Who knew? It could certainly get worse. The baby could get sick again and die. Cranes could stop falling out of the sky.

The sun fell inexorably toward the horizon. The air was pink. In the southern distance the Hindu Kush for the first time that day was becoming three-dimensional, slowly, like a print in a photographer's darkroom. Veiled by late-afternoon haze. Neither copper nor lavender nor blue. Some uncertain color. Like life and death in Afghanistan.

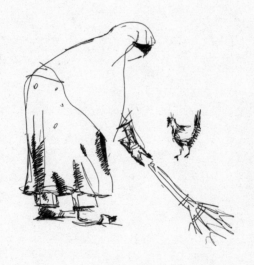

THE WEDDING

〜〜〜

The two-thirty a.m. to Kabul was operated by Bazarak Panjshir International Bus Transport Co. It was a white and scarlet fifty-seven-seat Mercedes-Benz decommissioned from Busverkehr Imfeld, a charter company established in 1946 in Landstuhl, Germany, though the bus itself had been assembled in the eighties. MIT UNS KOMMEN SIE AN! the former owner's motto proclaimed in firehouse red and gold from the side. Escape hatches were marked NOTAUSSTIEG. Above the driver's cabin, a sign instructed NO SMOKIN. Cardboard peaches of air freshener dangled from the handrails, and small plastic trashcans, untethered, slid about the floor of the aisle at each turn, each steep incline, each descent. There was no bathroom on board. Passengers had to buy tickets in advance at a kiosk near the Blue Mosque. The seats were numbered, and the seating was assigned.

The bus took on passengers and cargo at the Kabul Bus Terminal in southeastern Mazar-e-Sharif, where the Hindu Kush sloped toward the city in soft pleats of drab shale. The terminal was a vast patch of trampled dirt littered with empty and crushed plastic water bottles, goat droppings, susurrous tinsel of wrappers from Iranian biscuits, rotting peels of miniature Jalalabad bananas, human excrement, strips of cloth. The Mazaris called it "The Harbor." Subliminal memories of a sixty-thousand-year-old coastal journey out of Africa, pelagic dreams pressed into ephemeral figure eights by bus tires on a landlocked desert floor.

Most buses, like the Bazarak Panjshir International, left Mazar-e-Sharif before dawn. There were no streetlights. Gray dust danced and swallowed the short shafts of light from the bus headlights and the bus windows checkered the dirt into pale rhombi and the cigarette ends of drivers and hucksters carved small arcs in the night. Propane lamps blinked from within the tattered canvas wings of concession stands like dwarf stage lighting, and the stands themselves looked like puppet theaters some eccentric patron had ordered upon this grubby panorama. White pigeons cooed softly over pools of overnight piss. Sandaled porter boys materialized out of the black to grab at passengers' bags and usher the more tentative and lost-looking travelers into buses past a flock of sheep, maybe twenty head including a suckling lamb that, too, waited for their ride south. Mulberry wind buried the half-moon in smog. From the residential neighborhood to the north, the stuffy night carried the somnolent braying of donkeys, night watchmen's lonesome whistles, dreams. A boy with a red plastic shopping basket walked through the aisle of the bus calling, "Cake, biscuit, what do you want?" Behind him an old man carried small round flatbreads in a stack almost as tall as himself. The passengers dug in their pockets for change. "Here, *jan*!" "Come back here, *jan*!" "Give us those biscuits, *jan*." "Do you have any cold soda?"

A few minutes before the scheduled departure, a white minivan rolled up to the bus terminal. The minivan driver swung open the back doors and pulled out a long burlap sack. A name, a telephone number, and a Kabul address were written on the canvas in thick black marker. The man slung the bundle over his shoulder, lugged it to the bus, and heaved it through the open hatch of the baggage compartment. Inside the sack, wound into five tight scrolls, were five carpets.

Once Abdul Shakur, Baba Nazar's wool-and-carpet dealer in Dawlatabad, buys Thawra's carpet, he will call one of the carpet merchants in Mazar-e-Sharif to come and pick it up. In Mazar-e-Sharif, the merchant will send the carpet to be washed of bits of dung, particles of straw, and demoiselle crane feathers that might be stuck to the surface. Then he'll spread it on the floor of his dealership in Carpet Row, which fringes the eastern border of the Blue Mosque's rose garden like a strip of dark and expensive velvet, fold up a corner, and run his fingernail along the reverse side to evaluate the density of Thawra's weave. He will study the pile for the woman's inadvertent mistakes, a deep blue dot missing from a petal, a leaf along the ridge that suddenly blooms burgundy instead of scarlet, the slight deviation of a line—a journal of her months at the loom. An equation will form in his mind, a particular multiplication of knots by errors by square footage, and the carpet will be assigned a new price. If the merchant is preparing a large shipment of carpets that week, a hundred or more, he will fold the carpet pile side out and stack it in the corner of the shop until such a shipment is put together to be carried by truck either south to Kabul or west to Turkmenistan and on to one of the largest carpet bazaars in the world, in Istanbul. But if no truck shipment is on the horizon, he very likely will roll up Thawra's rug pile side in, stuff it into a burlap sack with four or five others, write the address of a sister dealership in Kabul on the sack, and assign a relative to take it to the bus terminal and get it into the cargo hold of a coach with a fancy English name such as Bazarak Panjshir International, or Kadrat Bus and Travel, or Hesarak Panjsher Bus Transport. For less than twenty-five dollars per bundle—about five dollars a rug—the bus driver will carry Thawra's carpet out of Bactria.

Eighteen minutes past schedule, the biscuit boy with the red shopping basket and the old baker disembarked and squatted on the curb to count their earnings by the rectangular lights cast by the bus windows. The passengers—a few women, wraithlike in their burqas, but mostly well-groomed businessmen headed to the capital in good leather shoes—shifted in their seats, muttered prayers. The bus was scheduled to arrive in Kabul at around ten in the morning, but it was always late. Some buses didn't make it there at all, but that, passengers and drivers agreed, was God's will.

The driver walked down the aisle to make sure each passenger had the correct seat and handed out thoughtful plastic bags, in case the travelers got carsick on the switchbacks. He was a Kabuli and looked like a washed-up rock star. Graying hair fell below his shoulders in greasy strands from under a brown crocheted skullcap, heavy silver rings shone on both hands, a silver brooch amulet was pinned to his vest. He had been a bus driver for thirty years, shuttling along the same route, Kabul–Mazar–Kabul. He made the journey three or four times a week. Each time he traveled south, he carried in his cargo hold a shipment of carpets.

At two-fifty the Bazarak Panjshir International sighed and

pulled out of the terminal. For the next thirty miles it pitched east-ward along Highway A76 through an empty steppe. "You traverse a country," Marco Polo wrote about this stretch of land, "that is desti-tute of every sign of habitation." An hour later, the road veered sharply to the south, where the Hindu Kush rose vertical, impene-trable, colossal. It rounded the upsloping pomegranate orchards of Tashqurghan, which at that dark hour trumpeted their scarlet blos-soms in secret, and the night-swallowed mound where in the sev-enth century the Chinese pilgrim Hsuan-tsang had described five hundred Buddhist monks living around ten temples. It squeezed almost impossibly through the barren Tashqurghan Gorge, where the layered and towering mountains cleft in a scarce chasm as if pried ajar by a crowbar; bounced past the unseen and gutted Soviet tanks buried in the oozing gravel of a freshet; and leveled onto the highland swells of Samangan, where dry riverbeds sheened in weak moonlight like ghosts of rivers frozen still in perfect mimicry of some singular moment of the water long gone, like unuttered screams.

At four-thirty the bus pulled over on top of a mountain pass so that the men on board could step outside to urinate and then to pray. They did both facing southwest toward Mecca, having un-wound their neckerchiefs and headscarves into makeshift prayer mats, although the driver had brought his own rug. The women remained stoically inside the bus and sat erect in absolute silence. By five in the morning, two-dimensional mountain peaks had begun to push against a murky orangeade sunrise in the east, and the bus was on its way again. Smells of Afghanistan wafted through the open roof hatches: manure, juniper fires, raw lamb fat. A man in the backseat began to sing sotto voce lovelorn Pashtun tunes, and in front, a woman prayed under her breath—*"Bismillah, bismillah"*—on every turn. There were many turns on the road.

"This road is much infested by highwaymen and it is unsafe to pass without an escort," Captain John Wood, the nineteenth-century Scottish explorer, reported from his journey here. Nearly two hundred years later, the highwaymen were still about, only they had morphed—into Taliban insurgents, roadside bandits, uniformed officialdom. Every dozen miles, the bus would stop at a checkpoint: a concrete bunker large enough to fit two stools and a propane burner for tea, maybe a boom barrier, or a length of rope pulled taut across the road at windshield height over a stretched-out disembodied tank tread. An officer in a gray fleece suit clutching a Kalashnikov by the barrel would slowly circle the bus and come up to the driver's window and stick out his free hand, into which the driver would press a couple of soiled banknotes. The exchange was almost always silent.

By six-thirty in the morning, the sun was blasting the highway full on, and the bus had heated up like a greenhouse. At seven fifty-five the heater switched on, unprompted. It would remain on until Kabul, even after the driver powered up the antiquated air conditioner. The broiling bus sped past the openwork lace of the caves of Dara-e-Suf, where Bronze Age men had molded animal figurines and Neolithic men before them had domesticated animals and, thirty-four thousand years ago, the *Homo sapiens* of the Upper Paleolithic had wielded hand axes made of flint. It overtook a maroon Toyota Corolla with a USMC sticker on the rear window and another Toyota Corolla stenciled with the larger-than-life image of the slain mujaheddin leader Ahmad Shah Massoud firing a Kalash-nikov assault rifle at tiny Soviet helicopters. A truck bejeweled with a giant heart of red-painted iron pierced with a giant arrow that dripped enormous, loaf-size drops of metal blood onto the rear fender. A flatbed truck full of stunned-looking cows. A petroleum truck emblazoned with a sign that warned ONE-WAY STREE. It rolled past a pumpkin patch not far from a massive temple built in the second century by the Kushan emperor Kanishka, where an old farmer slowly unbent to study the bus. In his right hand he held a serpentine vine in golden bloom. Past an unsettling scarecrow fash-ioned from an Adidas rain jacket with straw sticking out of the hood where a face would have been. Past rusting armored personnel carriers and distant armies of diffracted sheep. Rice fields mine fields battlefields. Somewhere below, a dozen inches off the ground, bounced the burlap bag of carpets.

Eight o'clock. Up nauseating switchbacks. (*"Bismillah, bismillah."*) Past chalky rapids and drowned rice paddies that shone cerulean blue like squares of upside-down sky and outcroppings of tank hulls that grew from creases in the mountainsides seamed with white veins of gypsum. Past roadside boys peddling purple and white mulberries from baskets handwoven out of mulberry branches that very morning. By eight-fifteen, from the muggy dustbowl of the Pul-e-Khumri River Valley the passengers spotted at last the black pancake of soot over the Salang Tunnel—the second-highest tunnel in the world, surpassed only by the Eisenhower Memorial Tunnel in the Rockies and rimmed with the baker's sugar of glacial ice.

Swallows danced in the galleries of Salang. The highway was narrow and the air coffee-colored with noxious diesel fog. The elevation was eleven thousand two hundred feet and it was cold, always. The snowdrifts on either side of the road were many winters old and absolutely black with exhaust. Nearly each year since Soviet engineers had bored into the mountains in the 1960s, travelers perished here in fires, in land-mine accidents, in avalanches. The blue coulee below was an ossuary of human remains and mangled metal. Hundreds of carpets that had never made it to Kabul draped the unmarked tombs of these ill-fated pilgrims.

And—down again. *"Bismillah, bismillah,"* came the burqa-stifled moans, the Pashtun singer retched into his bag, and outside the bus windows, the fast, cool stream of the Salang River, milky with late-spring snowmelt, rushed past the jade terraced fields of Jabal-us-Seraj. Turquoise and crimson dresses fluttered from clotheslines, and on the west bank a granite boulder the size of a farmhouse hung over a bend in the river. The boulder was split in two. I first saw it in 2001, the year of the American invasion, when I journeyed from the Khorasan on a newspaper assignment a few weeks behind the barefoot, vengeful, exalted army of victorious northern Afghan peasants, Washington's outsourced boots on the ground. The road at the time was an escapee from a Cormac McCarthy novel, a dull November porridge of sludge-filled ruts, a vaguely defined tract pulped into muck by hundreds of aerial bombs and furrowed by thousands of crisscrossing tank treads and kneaded by the feet of these ununiformed soldiers. These men, who would enter the capital and execute people—Taliban functionaries? Random men in dark turbans? Old foes?—and leave their bodies to rot in sludge-gorged

gutters, they must have seen the boulder then, too, from the road. Who knows how long it had been there, precarious, huge? Which shudder of Afghanistan's still-evolving orogeny had hurled it from the mountains and smashed it? Had it been here when Alexander the Great had built his fort, long since gone, in Jabal-us-Seraj? Whose histories hid in that crack, whose memories whispered into its igneous chill? Low stone houses had grown around the rock, and from the bus window the passengers watched sandaled children play with a deflated soccer ball.

The carpets rocked in the belly of the bus as it drove out of the mountains. White cumuli and Black Hawks soared above the Shomali Plain, above a cemetery of several hundred tanks and how-itzers, above the luminous tangle of vineyards in the valley horticul-turists know as the birthplace of table grapes, where more than a hundred and twenty varietals of the fruit once grew. It was almost noon by the time the Mercedes-Benz pulled up to the Parwan-e-Seh Bus Terminal in Kabul, a paved roundabout where remnants of dirty roses pushed through the litter in the median. After the pas-sengers had disembarked, the rock star driver dialed the local carpet merchant. He wasn't answering the phone. The driver dialed again, and again. No one picked up. The carpets would sit in the cargo hold maybe for the rest of the day, maybe longer.

⤳⤳⤳

Kabul? Ha! He's never even been to Tashqurghan!" Baba Nazar mocked his son. Baba Nazar himself had served in Tashqurghan in the army for a year. His recruit's salary had bought him lamb kebab every other day, and while he had not been issued a gun, the switch he had whittled for himself from a weeping willow had been sufficient to police the ancient streets that wound among the famous pomegranate groves. "Sometimes we'd use our belts to whip the people who misbehaved. That was enough to keep them afraid."

But that had been half a century earlier, way before Amanullah was born, back when Afghanistan had been ruled by a king and there had been plenty of deer to hunt with a bow and arrow right outside the pomegranate orchards, and even mountain lions that would slink down from the sawtooth peaks like shadows.

Neither Amanullah nor Baba Nazar had ever been to Kabul. They had never seen the green-tiled mosaic of rice paddies in Jabal-us-Seraj, the head-spinning abysses of Salang, the rich and warped embroidery of Shomali vineyards. But now the hunter's son was plotting a grand escape: he would come to Mazar-e-Sharif in Qaqa Satar's Toyota, ask the driver to drop him off at the bus terminal, and take a bus to Kabul from there. He would buy a fifteen-dollar ticket with his savings and ride in a cushioned and assigned seat and gorge his strabismic eyes on the land that would crumple and smooth out and rise vertiginously and drop again outside his window. He would try to not get carsick on the switchbacks. He would draw comfort from the knowledge that the familiar weave of carpets rode in the cargo hold beneath him. He even had figured out an excuse, which he confided in a loud whisper to four-year-old Leila on the *namad* rug rolled out in the glaring sun.

"I'll bring you back some shoes from Kabul," the man promised his daughter. And he pulled the laughing girl down into his lap and wrapped one of his enormous ticklish hands around both her ankles and proceeded to measure her wriggling feet with his thick fingers spread apart and tried to memorize the distance between them, for size.

But Baba Nazar said absolutely not, and once again Amanullah stayed home.

~~~~

It was May. Mynah birds had returned from a winter in India to hop in and out of open windows and doors, to sidle up to *dastarkhans* at mealtime and mimic the voices of diners and pry open with their yellow beaks any plastic bags that looked promising. In Zadyan, fat ripe mulberries tugged at the century-old churned branches and plopped softly upon the bone-colored dust, into the upturned shirttails of boys' *shalwar kameez*, into the juice-stained palms of girls. In Mazar-e-Sharif, the police were hunting for the six Taliban operatives from the south who a month earlier had instigated the massacre of the twelve United Nations employees. In an unpaved street a few blocks away from my house, four young boys had tripped a piece of Soviet ordnance and died in the explosion. In Pakistan, American special forces had killed Osama bin Laden, though very few villagers in the desert of northern Balkh Province had heard about the killing, certainly no one had in Oqa, where very few had heard anything about bin Laden at all. A few nights later, in Karaghuzhlah, Talibs on motorcycles had woken the village mullah to deliver two identical handwritten letters that announced that from then on the village belonged to the Taliban and had to pay the religious tax, *zakat*, to underwrite the militia's holy war effort. A heartfelt rain shower had emptied at last over Oqa, and some new hard greens had thumbed immediately through the salt pan and bloomed into a gossamer carpet of myriad tiny white stars. The rain had woken up diligent scarab beetles that pushed beads of dung the length of the hummock. It had dimpled the dunes and churned up the dust in the two village wells. Tea was cloudy for days. A sparrow had flown into Baba Nazar's house, and he and Amanullah had caught it and tied a string to its matchstick leg so that Nurullah could fly it around like a tiny live kite. The rip down the front of Boston's dress had frayed further and now showed her dark and withered right nipple. Amin Bai the Commander had quit smoking cigarettes. And Thawra had knotted about four more inches of the carpet since Nawruz: four more inches of burgundy and carmine geometric trees and angular scarlet and indigo flowers and stylized eagles in shades of red flying through rhombi of cobalt sky. Her progress was slowed, Baba Nazar explained, by all the weddings. Spring was wedding season in the Khorasan.

And now another wedding was coming up. On Sunday, Naim, the forty-year-old bachelor, would take at last into his small adobe his bride, the beautiful Mastura, the niece of Choreh. They had become betrothed three years earlier, when she was fourteen. He had paid her father, Choreh's brother, all of his savings for her hand—more than a thousand dollars. That was only a tenth of what Turkoman brides normally cost.

In patriarchal Afghanistan, marriages were always arranged and the birth of a son was always welcome. A daughter would grow up and marry and move to her in-laws' home, whereas a boy would ensure that his father's wealth remained within the family, and his wife and children would spare his aging parents from the hardest chores. In Turkoman families, the birth of a girl was almost equally embraced. In the calculated financial exchange that was marriage, a Turkoman girl fetched the highest bride price of all Afghan maidens because she could do more than keep house and raise children. She possessed a particular virtue. She could weave.

Lucky was the boy who had an older sister; she would wed first and he would use her bride price to marry his own wife. Naim, by far the oldest in his family, was not lucky. To defray the bride price, he turned to *badaal*—the poor man's practice of a bridal swap. In return for Mastura's hand he was giving away in marriage his little sister, Anamingli, to Mastura's brother, Ozyr Khul.

Anamingli was sixteen years old, graceful and tall. Two thick braids framed her moon-white face and ran past her marble neck fluid and glossy like a pair of mink. She had assembled a dowry of several *namad* rugs to line her floor in winter, a couple of *yusufi* carpets of burgundy and indigo wool to absorb the hungry cries of her future babies, several pillowcases embroidered with emerald and fuchsia blossoms and gold thread to gladden the eye of her guests, and two heavy flowered polyester blankets imported from China.

Ozyr Khul was slight and stood barely five feet off the ground. He always wore a pink skullcap and a dirty ecru *shalwar kameez*, the only set of clothes he owned. He didn't always wipe his nose. His best friends were twelve, eleven, and eight years old. When an adult addressed any one of them, the four boys would stand together in a mismatched row, arms draped over one another's shoulders. His favorite pastime was to run, alone and with his friends and in larger flocks of boys that dashed about Oqa like hosts of sparrows, like peppercorn scatterings, slingshots in hand. He was an expert shot at speckled desert birds, at distant rocks, at the amaranthine sky. A few days before his wedding, he had gotten into a wrestling match with a nine-year-old girl. He won.

Ozyr Khul himself did not know how old he was. One of his friends said he was thirteen, another suggested fifteen. His parents insisted he was sixteen, the legal marrying age in Afghanistan. Ozyr Khul's age and maturity were the subjects of animated discussions in the village during the long forenoons before the wedding, the butts of crude and unsparing ridicule.

"Do you like your fiancée, Ozyr Khul?"

"Ozyr Khul! When you are alone with your bride for the first time, what will you do?"

"He's too young to know how a woman is built—he'll end up doing it in the ass!"

"Well, let's find out. Hey, come here, Ozyr Khul! Tell us where you'll touch her on your wedding night!"

And the boy ran, ran, ran from his tormentors, dirty heels flashing over the hard-packed clay, sweaty palm clasping the trusted slingshot, his only ally in the whole wide world, the soiled pink skullcap blinking at the sun with all the *taweez* charms that his mother had sewn onto it over the years but that did nothing to protect him from having to grow up, suddenly, cruelly, this beautiful spring of the Afghan year 1390.

〜〜〜〜

Funerals were frequent in Oqa. Several times each year men trudged down to the gray cemetery south of the village to lean into the lonesome wind and stab the clay with their spades for a fresh grave. Just a few months earlier, Amin Bai the Commander had buried his two-year-old daughter there, under the brittle earth scaly with miniature drifts of hard gray dust. Over the nine unlucky years of their marriage, his neighbors, Abdul Khuddus and Oraz Gul, had buried all five of their girls—Fatma Gul, Gul Jamal, Najia Gul, Nuria Gul, and the infant who had been born dead and so had not been named. Who knew why the baby had been stillborn, why the others had wasted away? There was no doctor to ask for help, or for a postmortem.

But for many seasons now, weddings had bypassed this tiny and forgotten hamlet. The men of Oqa married girls in Khairabad and Karaghuzhlah, in Toqai and Zadyan, and brought them home after the nuptials. Oqa's girls married men from other villages and stayed there. Naim and Ozyr Khul's wedding to Mastura and Anamingli was going to be the first in Oqa in a decade. The whole village was getting ready.

Naim's family had invited musicians to come from Shor Teppeh and a mullah to come from Khairabad and was making arrangements with a Khairabad chef to cook veal pilau for all the guests. In the west of the village, where Ozyr Khul's family lived next to Amanullah and Choreh, women shifted their infants from one hip to another as they strung a sheet of dark-green cloth under the wattle-and-daub ceiling of the single-room house that was to be-

116

come the younger couple's honeymoon suite. Girls knotted garlands out of tinfoil candy wrappers and hung them from the roof beams. They made a curtain for the doorless entryway out of lurex headscarves. They built a pillow-size heart of red, silver, green, orange, and blue papier-mâché and nailed it to the western wall of the room to mark the spot where the newlyweds would lie together atop a narrow tick mattress.

Everything in the room sparkled. Even the pillows were embroidered with things shiny and sharp. Women and girls came and went, came and went past the shimmering silver-threaded door curtain to adjust a garland ring here, a tassel of a wool runner there. Men, too, ambled into the room to watch the decoration in progress, to click their tongues, to remark once again on the young groom's manhood.

"Looks nice, but it will be years before he knows what to do with her in it," said some.

"How pretty. What a waste," said the others.

Choreh stopped by. He surveyed the newlyweds' room and nodded his approval. Then he planted a sloppy mustachioed kiss on my cheek, and asked:

"Well? Have you found any aid for me in America?"

Hypotheses about my purpose in Oqa and my abilities and limitations wafted across the desert like sand, windblown and unreliable. In Khairabad they said that I was doing surveys (that was not true) and always writing something in my notebook (that was). In Karaghuzhlah, that I drank lots and lots of tea (true) and also that I was so strong I could kill two men with one arm. The latest apocrypha had come courtesy of Qaqa Satar, who had been telling people that I was a champion boxer—to discourage potential attackers, and also to justify the fact that I traveled unarmed. (Amanullah's invitation to wrestle in the dunes now had an explanation: he had wanted to test his physical prowess against my rumored super-human strength.) Amanullah told a cousin from Zadyan that I was going to tell the story of Oqa on the radio, like the journalists in Japan who were telling stories of the latest devastating tsunami. Occasionally, a visitor to Oqa would ask: "Is she building something here?" and Baba Nazar would respond: "No. She only takes notes and tells stories." And, to preempt potential requests for aid, he would add: "This woman can't do anything for us."

He was right. I was of no practical use whatsoever. I was an in-adequate raconteur, a collector of other people's joys and hardships. A mockingbird. A mynah bird. An echo. That I was welcome in the village, month after famished month, was entirely a measure of my hosts' inexhaustible magnanimity. Ultimately, this was what drew me: that I could show up burdened with deadlines, with the need to fill my notebook and with nothing to offer my hosts in return, and the next thing I knew, I was adopted into the family, mothered, fa-thered, fed, and loved with the kind of unconditional love that wrapped its tired hands tirelessly around me just because I was there, just because I had come, because in war and sorrow, love was the quintessence of defiance.

And if Choreh refused to see it that way, it was because he was a junkie in Oqa—the most incorrigible kind of a dreamer.

"Well?" I asked him, in turn. "Have you joined the army?"

"After the wedding, after the wedding," he replied, and waved me away with both his hands.

. . .

"I don't like this custom, exchanging brides," grumbled Baba Nazar. "It means that if Ozyr Khul hits his wife, Naim will have to hit his, tit for tat. Ozyr Khul isn't mature enough, he's too young to understand that getting married is a big responsibility."

But two of the hunter's children—his second daughter, Jamal, and his son, Amanullah—had married in a similar bridal swap, because Amanullah had spent most of whatever little money he had inherited from the marriage of his crippled older sister, Zarifshah Bibi, on whores in Mazar-e-Sharif.

Baba Nazar himself had been twenty-eight when he had married Boston. Boston had been eighteen. They were cousins. Like all marriages in Oqa, theirs had been arranged by their parents and focused on the merger of two estates, ensuring that the inheritance of both man and wife—a handful of goats, a couple of camels, some sheep long since eaten or sold—didn't go to strangers. It had not taken into consideration the wishes of the bride or the groom, though as far as the couple could recall, they had not found each other particularly repulsive at the time.

More than forty years had passed since. The same sun and dust had dried their skin, the same hungry months had shrunk their stomachs, the same progression of winters had gnawed at their bones. They had borne three children: Zarifshah Bibi, the oldest, who lived in Zadyan; Amanullah, who lived with them; and Jamal, who became Thawra's brother's second wife and lived with her husband, his first wife, and their children in a one-room house on the eastern edge of Oqa. Arthritis had cinched Boston's spine, and now she moved around unnaturally straight-backed. Baba Nazar had lost most of his teeth and much of his eyesight. The desert had weathered the old couple to look like siblings, and they chaffed like siblings as well.

"I'm broke, that's the problem. If I had money, I'd get married again," Baba Nazar would say. "My wife is too old for me now."

And Boston would laugh with her entire small body, and her gray braids would dance about her shoulders. Her wrinkles would fold and refold. Her necklace of keys would rip her old dress a little farther. And she would flick at her man with her smart old hands and say right in front of everyone: "Go! Shoo! Go! Go marry another woman! I'm tired of you, you old goat!"

But in the rare minutes when Boston was not mending an old homemade *chapan* coat or kneading dough or baking bread or helping Thawra weave or trying to rein in her grandchildren, and when Baba Nazar was not hunting rabbits in the desert or riding his donkey to market or poisoning cranes or entertaining guests, the two would sit next to each other on Baba Nazar's bed, the only bed in Oqa. Their bony buttocks would sag with the old springs. Their elbows would touch just barely. Their eyes would water together at the patient horizon in the kind of quietude that sometimes happens after a long marriage.

❧❧❧

Bactria's most famous nuptials also took place in late spring. That marriage, too, was arranged and focused on acquisition of wealth: Alexander the Great, at twenty-nine the king of Macedon, *shahanshah* of Persia, lord of Asia, pharaoh of Egypt, and still a bachelor, defeated Oxyartes, the prosperous ruler of Balkh, and took his daughter, Roxane, to be his wife. She was sixteen years old and, in the words of the Greek historian Arrian of Nicomedia, "the loveliest woman in Asia, with the exception of the wife of Darius," the former king of Persia, another of Alexander's vanquished foes.

The year was 327 BC. The wedding took place in the majestic city-state of Balkh—the Avesta's "beautiful Bakhdhi with high-lifted banner," the fourth creation of the Zoroastrian god Ahura Mazda and the home of Zoroaster; the Bakhtri of the Achaemenids; the Baktra of the Greeks.

For fifteen hundred years, Balkh dominated Central Asia from a valley that dropped away from the bajadas of the Hindu Kush in swirls of fecund color. "The ornament of all Ariana," Strabo, the first-century Greek philosopher and historian, wrote in *Geographica*, his seventeen-volume opus. "Plentiful trees and vines provide abundant crops of succulent fruits," wrote his Roman contemporary Quintus Curtius Rufus in *Historiae Alexandri Magni*. "The rich soil here is irrigated by numerous springs and the more fertile parts are sown with wheat . . . After that a large area of the country is engulfed by desert sands."

Two thousand years later,

a knoll in that "desolate and arid region," about thirty miles northeast of Balkh, would become Oqa.

After the Kushans had annexed it in 128 BC, Balkh developed into a major crossroads on the Great Silk Road. Merchants from China arrived to trade rubies and furs and aromatic gums and silk with Indian traders of spices and cosmetics and ivory, with Roman salesmen of gold and silver vessels and wine. Carpets woven by local women traveled in every direction. Three hundred monks prayed at a hundred monasteries and temples before Buddha statues adorned with precious stones. "This is a country truly privileged," marveled the Chinese monk-scholar Hsuan-tsang. When the Arabs invaded in AD 645, they called Balkh the Mother of All Cities, Umm al Belaad. "It was in the Eastern lands as Mecca is in the West," wrote Ala ad Din Ata Malik Juvaini, the Persian-born annalist of the Mongol Empire. In the tenth century, Rabia Balkhi, the first woman known to compose poetry in both Arabic and Persian, compared her city to a garden abrim with flowers. Eleven hundred years later, women still came to weep and pray beside her tomb in the heart of the city.

Then, in 1220, Genghis Khan led one hundred thousand horsemen on Balkh.

The slaughter was mythical, the devastation absolute. Helmed by a psychopathic leader who at the age of ten had killed his half brother, the nomads sat their mounts like centaurs and fought like death incarnate. They smothered horses with grease rendered from the bodies of prisoners and lit them afire and set them upon enemy lines. They carried bubonic plague and put to the sword any city-state that refused to submit to slavery. They slaughtered a tenth of the world's population. Within two centuries, the Mongols would rule a khanate that stretched from the Black Sea to the Sea of Japan and was poised to engulf Western Europe. By the mid–thirteenth century, when, in the words of Sir Winston Churchill, "Germany and Austria at least lay at their mercy," court intrigue and divisions within their own massive imperium would halt their advance. The Golden Horde would turn around and rush to the Mongolian capital at Karakorum to elect a new khan in place of Ogedei, Genghis Khan's third son and successor to his rule, who had either drunk himself to death or had been poisoned with fermented horse milk. The Horde would leave behind wreckage, the Black Death, and gunpowder.

In Balkh the Mongols spared no woman, man, or child. There was no one to bury the dead. "For a long time the wild beasts feasted on their flesh, and lions consorted without contention with wolves, and vultures ate without quarreling from the same table with eagles," Juvaini wrote. "And they cast fire into the gardens of the city and devoted their whole attention to the destruction of the outworks and walls and mansions and palaces . . . And wherever a wall was left standing, the Mongols pulled it down and . . . wiped all the traces of culture from the region." Fifty years after the massacre, Marco Polo reported that "Balach, a large and magnificent city" had "sustained much injury from the Tartars, who in their frequent attacks have partly demolished the buildings." A century after Genghis Khan had sacked Balkh, the Arab traveler Ibn Battuta described it so: "It is now in ruins, and without society."

The city never recovered. In 1832, Sir Alexander Burnes, advisor to the British ambassador in Kabul, saw "fallen mosques and decayed tombs, which have been built of sun-dried brick . . . The city itself, like Babylon, has become a perfect mine of bricks for the surrounding country."

On a Friday before Ozyr Khul and Naim married each other's sisters, a friend invited me to ride horses in Balkh.

We drove from Mazar. A police checkpoint and a tank-tread speed bump beneath a gnawed stump of a bimillenary wall denoted the southern gate. From it, a paved road ran straight for a mile or so to a dingy park in the city center. In the northeastern corner of the park, a lofty arch still plastered in spots with tiles of turquoise and indigo glaze was all that remained of the madrassa of Sayed Subhan Quli Khan, a seventeenth-century college. Directly to its west, minarets corkscrewed above the tattered and defaced domed octagon of Masjid-e-Sabz, the Green Mosque, built five or six centuries earlier in memory of the Balkh theologian Khojah Abu Nasr Parsa. "Unsubstantial and romantic," Robert Byron wrote of the mosque in May of 1934; it stood in disrepair already then. "An unknown force seems to be squeezing it upwards. The result is fantasy, and in some lights, an unearthly beauty."

From the simple iron fence that girdled the park, some carpets hung. Patinated with road dust like the severe faces of the dealers who squatted in the dirt beneath them. These were the rejects: the thicker-wooled, fewer-knotted, simpler cousins of Thawra's *yusufi*, the carpets Mazari dealers would not buy. Their clumsy threads were echoes of greatness, their pile the shadows of the carpet King Alexander was said to have sent to his mother from this conquered

city. But their reds were just as
rich as the blood that had nour-
ished Balkh to its former maj-
esty, that had plunged it into its
present demise.

Eroded stubs of the de-
spoiled and ancient walls pro-
truded like the exposed ribs of
a giant carcass among nonde-
script streets of partly shuttered
storefronts and simple mud
homes that rayed from the park.
Few people walked those streets. Oxyartes, the Balkh ruler who
had yielded the city to Alexander the Great, had had under his
command thirty thousand cavalrymen when about two hundred
million people had lived on Earth. Now, in the world of seven billion souls, the entire population of Balkh was fewer than eight
thousand people.

A citadel unimaginatively called Bala Hissar, the Citadel,
marked the city's northern boundary. The fort's thick crenellated
fifteenth-century ramparts melted like candle wax onto the first-
century foundation that draped over substructures of clay and mud
brick laid here three hundred years before Alexander's wedding.
Below the walls, fields and orchards fanned out in all directions:
puffs of apricot trees already gray with dust, drowned rice paddies
like spalls of glass, fields of yellow-black okra flowers unblinking at
the sun. Girls in long scarlet shawls squatted among the miniature
silver fireworks of onion blossoms. To the north, fields blued into

the distant desert. To the south, the shorn Hindu Kush slept, smoky and still.

Who is the fourth that rejoices the Earth with greatest joy? Ahura Mazda answered: "It is he who sows most corn, grass, and fruit, O Spitama Zarathushtra! who waters ground that is dry, or drains ground that is too wet. Unhappy is the land that has long lain unsown with the seed of the sower and wants a good husbandman, like a well-shapen maiden who has long gone childless and wants a good husband."

—Vendidad

This was the land the itinerant monk Hsuan-tsang had beheld, and King Alexander before him, and Zarathushtra before them both. The manmade glory of the city may have vanished under the sword of men. But the people of Balkh, barefoot, unbeaten, with wooden hand ploughs, rejoiced their land, forever.

The horse drivers waited for Friday customers inside Bala Hissar. They were Uzbek—the descendants, some scholars believed, of Genghis Khan's son Juchi. They stood inside the fort's walls smoking and shucking sunflower seeds. Their horses, the fluid and slim Akhal-Tekes, like Alexander's Bucephalus and the warrior-horses of Genghis Khan, were grazing on some chamomiles. Fifty paces away, in a niche by a mulberry tree contorted over a hand pump, veiled women prostrated themselves beneath the harlequin flags of the shrine of Pahlawan Ahmad Zimchi, a heroic warrior whose story no one any longer could remember precisely other than that he had been preternaturally strong. The pilgrims prayed to the *pahla-*

wan to impart some of his strength to their sons and took off their hair bands and ribbons and the cheap bangles of painted aluminum that bazaar Gypsies sold for a penny and kissed them and whispered prayers to them and kissed them again and placed them on the pale bricks of the shrine. The shrine glittered with trinkets. The horse drivers kept their backs to the women, out of modesty.

I rented a bay gelding from a man without a leg.

"A small circle around the water pump or a big circle around the ramparts?"

"A big circle."

"Seven hundred afghanis."

"You're kidding! It's less than a kilometer around. One hundred."

Haggling was always expected, but I felt badly about bargaining with a man with a peg leg. He said he had lost his own in war. Which war, he did not specify. War in general.

"Two-fifty."

"Okay."

"Do you want me to walk in front of you and lead the horse?"

"Oh, no, thank you."

"Well, suit yourself."

We ambled. Slow. Hooffall to hooffall with Genghis Khan's horsemen above the green plains. Riding atop the land where the Golden Horde had sacked the Mother of All Cities. The walls of Balkh, those ancient sepultures, keened under the bay's small hooves with the trampled laments of all the dead. Indian rollers tumbled bluely out of the heavens like swatches torn out of the sky and somersaulted over the fields of onions in cloudlike bloom.

But the horses of Bala Hissar had been trained not to walk far-ther than a hundred and fifty meters away from their owners, like circus ponies. After a minute, my gelding—it had no name and had responded, up to this point, to *"prrrr-prrrr"* and *"ch'k-ch'k-ch'k"*—stopped irresolute for a few beats, then turned around and trudged at a slow gait back to its master, who was now laughing openly at my foolhardy assumption that for five dollars he would let me ride away on his beautiful steed.

~~~

When I was leaving, the one-legged jockey shouted: "Hey, foreign lady!"

I turned. He flew up into the saddle in one liquid motion and raised his sweaty leather crop and grinned and leaned forward and whispered something to his horse and the horse reared, and for a mo-ment that seemed to last centuries they stood like that in the bronze May light, sparkling and vertical against the long horizons of Bac-tria, the man and his mount as one, their thickly veined necks strain-ing together for the heavens, the rider no longer a seed-shucking cripple whoring out his horse to weekend tourists but a mischievous demiurge, a ghost of Genghis Khan, perhaps, or Tengri the Sky God himself, awesome and magnificent, a monument to the countless cav-alries that had slaughtered and been slaughtered upon this very land.

Then he brought the horse back down and whooped once, and they loped over the battlements and out of sight into the haze-choked valleys, the horse and its eternal rider picking their way past the pendular swings of immemorial, internecine violence.

. . .

"Ordinary people here treat political cataclysms—coups d'état, military takeovers, revolutions, and wars—as phenomena belonging to the realm of nature," wrote the Polish journalist Ryszard Kapuściński. He was describing life in Zanzibar during the revolution in 1964. He could have been describing life on the war-littered pan of the Khorasan, any given year.

War itself here aligned with the elements. It climaxed between the blooming of almonds and the harvesting of pomegranates, when the persistent sun of late spring and summer unlocked the subarctic mountain passes and stilled the brown veins of gravelly snowmelt and smoothed the white roadless desert into the widest road imaginable, a salt-caked craquelure that blinded and stung and suffocated by day, but by night exhaled the accumulated heat in soft, windblown caresses upon whichever men bore arms that season. Upon the nineteenth-century guerrillas wielding *jezail* matchlocks against the British Raj in the romantic crescent light of the moon. Upon the twentieth-century anti-Soviet mujaheddin. And, the year of Ozyr Khul's wedding, upon the turbaned and masked motorcycle riders of the Taliban.

Methodical and unobstructed, and mostly without a shot, the Taliban laid claim to the villages that spread from Balkh in paisley daubs of fruit gardens and leas. Karaghuzhlah, where two of the demoiselle cranes Baba Nazar had poisoned out of the clouds stood sentinel among wooly sheep and scrawny chickens in the yard of a small-time warlord. Zadyan, where the hunter's daughter, Zarifshah Bibi, lived with her disfigurements, her ancient husband, and her two small children. Karshigak, where Abdul Shakur the wool dealer colored his yarn with the root of wild madder and synthetic dyes from Pakistan. Khairabad, where Oqa's boys and men went to barter calligonum for rice and whole-wheat flour. Through a breach in Bala Hissar's western wall you could see, here and there, a black Taliban flag flutter above an orchard. At least one flew in Khoja Aqa Shah-e-Wali, a village where we stopped on the way from the fort. This village was best known for a mosque engirdled by a vast garden of centennial mulberry trees that in May stood heavy with fruit, pale yellow and purple like coagulated blood.

A hundred trees must have grown there on a grid. Families and groups of young men and separate groups of delicate schoolgirls in inadequate heels lounged under the shady branches on homespun blankets. Slender sapphire coils of smoke curled past the trunks from a kebab grill somewhere and among the leaves a thousand birds sang and the fresh sky above the orchard shone like a vault of polished glass. I bought a small packet of cold mango juice from a vendor's icebox and picked berries off the trees. Denuding the branches as if I were a goat until my belly felt very sweet, and that made me laugh, and the families I passed smiled and waved and settled back to their picnics because, Taliban or not, it was Friday.

> *Come to the orchard in Spring.*
> *There is light and wine, and sweethearts*
> *in the pomegranate flowers.*
> *If you do not come, these do not matter.*
> *If you do come, these do not matter.*
>
> —RUMI

. . .

The Taliban came to Oqa that May, as well. They came at night and revved their motorcycles in the moon-blued dust and had a word with Amin Bai the Commander and left. I asked the Commander what they had talked about. "Life," he said. He would say no more. They brought no flags, took nothing, and staked no land claims.

"We are of no use to them," Amin Bai would say later. "We are too far from everything."

~~~

The day before the wedding, a sedate stillness fell over the village. Hot sun had wrung all color out of the sky and along the faded horizons whitecap clouds lay static like the white trim of a prayer rug. Across the iambic plains the hours stretched syrupy and swollen by the heat.

Mid-morning, the Prophet Mohammed floated out of the nacreous desert astride the Buraq, the heavenly winged beast.

For a minute the rider and his mythical mount pranced through molten air, huge and diffracted and veering in the rising heat. Then they shrank and touched down, and the rider became Baba Nazar and his ride the hunter's gray donkey and its wings panniers stuffed to overflowing with skeletonweed, animal feed the old man had picked on his way home from Khairabad, where he had been visiting with a relative and where green and tepid sludge still pooled in irrigation ditches. The hunter unsaddled the burro, hitched it to the artillery shell casing dug into the ground outside the loom room, heaped the feed by the iron bed, and went indoors to sweat in the shade of his house.

Where Boston and Thawra were preparing lunch in the kitchen.

The kitchen stove was a pair of conical clay ovens raised out of the dirt floor next to each other and severed open at the vertexes, each with room inside for a small kindling fire and a side opening through which to feed it. On one of them the quartered leg of a two-month-old kid Baba Nazar had slaughtered the day before hissed in a grimy pressure cooker. The walls above the stove were hung with dusty jerry cans and dusty pitchers and dusty burlap sacks sagging with something, everything dusty and held up by sticks driven into the mud walls. The low ceiling was grass thrown on top of uneven wooden beams. A single phosphorescent ray of sun, like a white and coruscating column, did not beam down through a gap in the roofing but rose upward to it from a blackened water pitcher on the floor. By that alien and solid shaft of light Boston and Thawra squatted, their faces in a Vermeer glow, frying onions in a large black wok, peeling and cutting potatoes over an aluminum basin, working in comfortable silence, in a timeworn synergy much older than their kitchen or their village. A pair of acolytes of an ancient order, the order of hearth keepers.

Lunch was served in Amanullah's bedroom on the old houndstooth *dastarkhan*. The steaming lava of Boston's goat and potato stew, heaped upon a large round pewter tray, drowned in oily onion puree colored scarlet by a dollop of tomato paste from a can I had brought from Mazar-e-Sharif, because tomato paste was a luxury in the village. Two loaves of whole-wheat nan, craggy and misshapen like Oqa's own hummock, their crusts so hard they rang when tapped with a fingernail, their crumb warm and soft and moist and slightly sour and earthy like a grandmother's embrace. A small chipped porcelain bowl of fresh camel-milk yogurt, spumy, cloudlike. The green thermos with pale hot tea. We pinched scalding strings of meat out of the stew with burning fingertips and shared a single aluminum spoon to take turns with the yogurt. No one spoke. It was one of those meals that strike you aphasic, that you remember later not with your tongue but with your very diaphragm. Every meal Boston cooked was like that.

"What, this?" Baba Nazar said when, later, I bowed to his wife in gratitude. "Pah! I could have cooked this myself!"

And Boston, who was sitting on the wooden threshold with her elbows on her knees and her palms cupping her cheeks, laughed and waved her hands at him and said: "Great! Go! Go to the kitchen! You'll be the cook tomorrow!"

But she knew she really couldn't call his bluff. Because tomorrow was wedding day in Oqa, and someone else was preparing lunch.

~~~

The wedding chef came by *zaranj* at dawn. His name was Jan Mohammad. He was an older brother of Abdul Rashid, Oqa's most desperate heroin addict, who often weaved through the village with dull bruised eyes, thin and blueskinned, listing under some drug-induced weight. Jan Mohammad was serious, stout, established-looking, and lived in Khairabad, where he had a big family and owned a few fields. With him he had brought to Oqa two young apprentices, three broad shovels with wooden handles, two thin brown *patu* blankets of fine sheep's wool, one washed-out muslin bedsheet, one sheet of black tarpaulin, and one five-hundred-gallon cast-iron vat, the same kind wool dyers used to stain carpet yarn. The vat was encrusted with generations of black grease on the outside and came with three dozen dinged pewter serving trays that had been scoured absolutely, surreally spotless. The chef ordered the *zaranj* driver to deliver all this to the northern edge of the village, not far from where Naim's bull camel had serviced a Toqai cow that winter—the best spot, all in Oqa agreed, for a morning of industrial-scale cooking.

Jan Mohammad's assistants dug a shoulder-deep pit, built a calligonum fire in it, and lowered the vat onto the fire. Into the vat they emptied two five-liter jerry cans of oil and, when that came to a smoky boil, a bushel of quartered onions, four kilos of veal in creamy-pink chunks each the size of a fist, seventeen and a half kilos of rice, and enough buckets of well water to cover the lot. By six-thirty in the morning, the scent of stewed onions and meat inundated every corner of Oqa. It twisted and pulled at the stomachs of the villagers and the men began to congregate around the fire pit, though a sense of decorum kept the women from joining. On a fire nearby, ten crane-necked pitchers of water were boiling for tea, and a few steps away, a group of young men were performing the redundant task of washing the impeccably clean serving trays with bunches of straw in a basin of murky well water. Beyond them, dappled with a chain of identical oval cloud shadows, the dunes sang.

Ralph A. Bagnold, the British troubadour of sand, has described

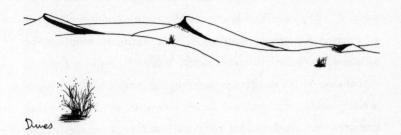

Dunes

the rare hummed canticle as "the great sound which in some remote places startles the silence of the desert." Bagnold had dedicated years to researching the behavior of desert sand in the ergs of Libya and in a personal wind tunnel he had built in England, and published his observations in 1941 in one elegant volume titled *The Physics of Blown Sand and Desert Dunes.* Yet even to this scholar who had scrutinized the anatomy of dunes grain by grain, the mechanics of the song remained a mystery. The chapter on singing dunes is the book's last. It ends thus: "Much more work will have to be done before the 'song of the sands' is understood."

But in Oqa everyone understood: the dunes were singing a wedding song that morning.

Meanwhile, wedding guests arrived.

They had come from Khairabad and Karaghuzhlah, from Toqai and Zadyan. Warlords. Farmers. Merchants. Drug dealers. All relatives of the Oqans—brothers, sisters, third cousins, nieces. Some had arrived by donkey and motorcycle. Most had walked. A few families had rattled across the cracked desert in the flatbeds of *zaranj* motor-rickshaws. Someone even had hired a taxi from Mazar-e-Sharif. They bore wedding gifts of pewter serving trays, plastic pitchers, aluminum washbasins. By seven in the morning, the village had swelled to six or seven hundred people embracing, exchanging kisses and gossip, laughing, sharing their latest heartaches, pinching the cheeks of babies born since the last time they had seen one another. Men thronged toward the northern slope where the pilau was cooking. Women and girls took over the south and west of the hummock.

The women in their holiday embroidery twinkled like mermaids accidentally cast upon these landlocked sands. Two and a half dozen had crowded into Boston's room, barefoot and lipsticked and glistening in unimaginable combinations of greens and blues and purples and pinks, and festooned with beads and sequins. All wore rouge. They dabbed sweat off their faces with the fringes of their brilliant scarves and shared two cigarettes, which they passed around clockwise, from one set of lips fuchsia or red or shiny oyster-blue to the next. They inhaled with somber concentration and tapped the ashes with elaborate hand flourishes on the straw mat that covered the earthen floor. Intricate henna flowers vined up their wrists from fingertips stained a deep brown. Most wore silver or gold jewelry in their ears and some in their noses and all on their fingers and wrists and necks. They had tuned Baba Nazar's radio to an AM music station from Turkmenistan, and a few girls were swaying their hips, and the colored reflections of their sequins rebated off the walls like strobe lights in a disco. Thawra leaned against the wall in a crimson gown. Next to her, Choreh Gul, her beaked smile carmine with lip gloss, clutched the infant Zakrullah. The boy's translucent thighs were bare and rounded at last with some fat. Little Leila wove around past these scintillating apparitions in loops—"I'm turning I'm turning I'm turning I'm turning!"—and steadied herself against their silken and glittering knees, and Boston, radiant in a shift of lurexed puce, wagged an index finger at her granddaughter and giggled. In the evening, the women said, musicians would come from Shor Teppeh, and the whole village would bloom like a bouquet of thistles into interlocking hoops of circle dances.

Anamingli was there as well, in a pinkish gown embroidered with silver beads and tiny flecks of tin that looked like fish scales. She did not dance. Perhaps she felt resentful about marrying a grimy boy three years her junior. Perhaps she was pleased. It was hard to say. Custom demanded that she look solemn on the day she left her parents' house no matter how she felt about it, and she did. She did not speak and did not smile and nodded at visitors with an air of profound importance. Her cheeks and forehead were talced and rouged and there were sparkles on her forehead and her eyes were contoured with kohl and shadowed pink that faded inexpertly into turquoise blue like some wild sunset, and beneath that makeup her teenage face was already lined with desert hardship. She had painted her lips bloodred.

Amanullah peeked into his mother's room and the bright maquillage of the women stung him deeply.

"For a wedding they'd do this!" he complained in a loud whisper. "But for their own husbands—never! Our women stay at home all day and still they don't wear makeup or jewelry for us. Several times I have bought lipstick for my wife, because I want her to be sexy, but she doesn't use it. I think they are just lazy."

Amanullah and I walked toward the pilau vat. Boys, as boys are wont to do, dashed everywhere. Among them, in his pink skullcap and his tan *shalwar kameez*, slingshot in sweaty hand as always, ran Ozyr Khul.

Halfway across the village, Choreh intercepted us. He nodded to Amanullah and slapped me very hard on my shoulder and kept his hand there awhile.

"I have no money," he announced. His tone accusing. His hand squeezing my shoulder with great force. His eyes wild, restless, leaning into mine.

"I know," I said. "You said you'd get a job after the wedding."

"That's right, that's right." And he let go of me and ambled away.

At seven-thirty, the chef and his apprentices stood at the lip of the fire pit and leaned over the vat and stirred the wedding pilau with shovels. They scooped it up from the bottom of the vat and turned it the way farmers would turn soil for sowing season and picked out bladefuls of burned rice and dropped them into an aluminum bowl to feed to the livestock later. When the rice and the meat and the onions were mixed together to Jan Mohammad's liking, the cook invited Baba Nazar to season the pot. With ceremony, the old man reached into a white plastic bag with both his hands and brought up a mound of powdery salt and tossed it in all at once. The apprentices then laid serving trays upside down to cover the rice, spread the bedsheet on top of that, covered it with the *patu* blankets, and then with the black tarp. They tucked in the blankets with their fingertips and patted them down with the flats of their palms. Gently. The way a mother might tuck in a child. There may have been no love in the nuptials that day, but the cooking was done with love.

Hair-dryer wind blew. Men sat outside on straw mats and *namad* rugs, perspiring and squinting against airborne dust, sipping tea from glass cups, refilling them, passing them around, talking. On a rug nearest the pilau vat, a group of men led by Naim was bidding on camels. They leaned into one another and shouted and threw fists in the air and swore—*"Bismillah!"*—and brought their fists down upon their friends' shoulders both to congratulate them on deals well made and to chide them for lousy sales. On the mat where I was sitting with Baba Nazar, a young man from Khairabad named Hasadullah was pondering a second marriage and making inquiries that, in his mind, could help slash the bride price before such a price was even announced. A kind of preliminary bargaining. The object of his interest was I.

"She doesn't work, that's why she's so thin," Hasadullah said.

"She says she works."

"Yeah, she's always writing something down."

"Then she only works with her brain."

He studied me, critical, appraising.

"Can she at least run?"

Hasadullah had a tattoo of two crossed scimitars on his right wrist ("I got it before I knew that tattoos were un-Islamic"), a wife, and three daughters—six, four, and two years old. "He is a future rich man," the other men joked. "God willing, he marries them well." Now he was silent again, making some calculations. He considered my city clothes: a knee-length shirt, trousers, a large headscarf. At last he asked: "What does she do when she wants to pee in the desert? Here, women have long skirts."

"We don't know."

"We've never seen her pee."

"She probably has to walk farther away than most."

Hasadullah pressed on.

"In America," he said, "in America, do you also pay money to marry?"

"No."

"Ah. Then if I come to America, I can marry for free?"

"Yes, but you'll run into a different problem. In America, people aren't allowed to have more than one wife, and you're already married."

"You could get a divorce," someone offered.

"No way! I paid almost ten thousand dollars for my wife!"

"How can anyone afford to marry here?" I whispered to Abdurrakhman, the young man pouring my tea. He had come to the wedding on foot from Karaghuzhlah, where he volunteered as a nurse at a Red Crescent clinic. When he had been a refugee in Pakistan during the Soviet occupation, he had decided to join the jihad and enrolled in a training camp for mujaheddin—a camp that probably had been sponsored by the CIA, and maybe by Osama bin Laden as well. He had attended long enough to learn how to administer injections. Then the Soviet troops pulled out of Afghanistan, the camp shut down, and Abdurrakhman never became a mujahed. He was still single.

"We can't," he whispered back. "That's why we swap brides."

An old mullah who had slumped against a mud wall overheard us and pursed his lips. The thick white turban of a hajji shaded his rheumy eyes, and sweat beaded on his shaved upper lip and sparkled in his sparse white beard. The mullah was a learned man and disapproved of the whole *badaal* business. Naim had paid him to come from Khairabad in a motor-rickshaw to bless two marriages that in the mullah's mind were barely legitimate.

"These people live in the desert," muttered the cleric. "They don't go to the mosque. They do whatever they want. They don't follow Shariah."

And without looking, he reached behind his shoulder and with long and manicured fingers flicked a little pale lizard off the wall.

The warlord who was reclining next to Baba Nazar was chewing *naswar*. He had ridden a motorcycle from Karaghuzhlah. His full name was Jan Mohammad, like the chef's, but everyone called him Janni. He was half Uzbek and half Tajik, in his thirties, tall, dark, bearded, and incredibly beautiful. Like a prince from a Mogul miniature. He traveled with bodyguards.

"Are you guys weaving a carpet?" he asked the hunter.

"Yes."

"How big?"

"Three meters."

"Three by two?"

"Three by one."

"So, like a runner?"

"Yes."

"When do you think it will be finished?"

"I don't know, the women haven't woven for fifteen days. At this rate, they may not be finished until fall."

Choreh stumbled up and Janni rose to his feet to greet him. As they embraced, Choreh felt the warlord's vest pockets for cash.

❧❧❧

The wedding pilau was done, and the chef and his apprentices set about to undress the vat. They lifted the tarp gently and laid it on the ground first. They laid the hot and soggy blankets on top of the tarp, then the muslin cloth on top of the blankets, then the scalding serving trays on top of the cloth. The rice was pellucid and golden, and seemed to glow. Jan Mohammad the chef patted it with the flat of his shovel blade and the pilau quivered like the breast of a young bride. Then he stabbed it deep and hoed and raked it for a few minutes until he had picked out all the meat, which he heaped onto a separate tray. At least one chunk of tender veal would rest upon a cushion of rice on each serving platter, and at every mat or carpet or mattress, the eldest diner would strip the meat apart with his or her hands into gelatinous strands no thicker than a pinkie so that each wedding guest got a bite. When there was nothing in the vat but rice and pulpy onions, the chef nodded to the elders. Baba Nazar approached, and the mullah from Khairabad, and Amin Bai, and Sayed Nafas, and several others. They stood in a semicircle, and the wind whipped their loose clothes around their knees and ankles, and tore tongues of steam off the rice and the meat, and stretched and balled the fragrant steam, and carried it off to the lowing dunes where it blurred into the runnels of sand forever drifting eastward. On the mats and blankets around the vat, all conversation and bargaining ceased. The elders stood very still and formal, and opened their palms to the heavens and lowered their heads to the ground overlaid with animal dung and pottery shards and feathers and in silence asked that God bless the food and the day and the two marriages. When they were finished, they passed their hands over their faces in benediction and uttered *"Bismillah"* and beckoned some young boys who would bus the food to the male guests first, then to the women. The chef and his helpers began to shovel the pilau onto the serving trays. It was nine-thirty in the morning on a Sunday in late May in Afghanistan.

The young groom, Ozyr Khul, was nowhere to be found.

〜〜〜

The musicians never showed up.

"They were afraid," said Amin Bai. He paused, and added, to clarify: "Of the Taliban."

Six months earlier, in Toqai, Taliban gunmen had opened fire during a wedding because there had been live music and dancing. Now musicians avoided traveling to weddings in villages they did not know well, whose security they could not vouch for. No one came to strum the twangy goat-gut strings of a *rubab* at the wedding of Naim and Ozyr Khul to Mastura and Anamingli. No one came to amuse their guests with the alternating lonesome wails and shrill cheer of the apricot-wood *tuiduk*, the flute Archangel Gabriel once had used to breathe soul into the clay body of Adam.

"No one wants to come here," the Commander said. To underline the severity of his proclamation, he fished a harsh Korean cigarette from the chest pocket of his vest, stuck it between his teeth, and lit a match to it. He had started smoking cigarettes again. His abstinence from tobacco had lasted five days. He counted them out on his chapped fingers and held up the fingers to the diaphanous Khorasan sky as if calling upon the sky's witness. Five.

And so it fell to the women to make music that wedding day. Modesty and custom demanded that the women party separately from the men, and to protect their dignity, no cell phones were allowed in Oqa during the wedding. It had become common for Afghan men to record videos of wedding dances on their cell phones and send them to one another by text, but some people considered such videos indecent. Several years earlier in Toqai, relatives of a bride shot to death two male guests for videotaping the wedding party. In Kabul, wedding photographers were receiving death threats.

The women had staked out the south-facing bank of the hummock that sloped down from the homes of Baba Nazar and Choreh and the new house of Ozyr Khul and Anamingli, and had strung some blankets and bedsheets between the adobes to fence off themselves from the ogling of the men. Within that provisional enclosure, they were in constant motion. Like a cageful of restless firebirds. They had dialed up the volume on Baba Nazar's radio to the maximum setting and clapped their hands and ululated and sang and laughed and banged out a syncopated, urgent rhythm on goatskin tambourines called *doyra*. They held the tambourines over their heads and in front of their sequined breasts and at their glittering hips, and turned in an undulating circle, tossing their bare heads and letting their unbraided hair cascade like mountain rivers unimagined in this desert, each girl and woman an explosion of all the dreams and all the stars that would draw across the sky that night. Hot wind whirled their music through the village and past the ears of the men and out into the dunes, which had fallen silent in the face of such extravagant reverie.

The men were swatting at wasps and picking at deep-fried pancakes of slightly sweet dough shaped like shoe soles and nodding their heads to the beat of the women's *doyra* when a group of dusty children led by Hazar Gul, Choreh's daughter, stormed into their midst and prodded Ozyr Khul forward. He was deep red in the face and very small in his fuchsia skullcap.

Busted.

Three older men rose from their mats and stood above him. Like guardians or vultures or maybe a little bit of both. Each two heads taller than the boy. The men held him gently by the shoulders, and one of them took from his sweaty hand his only prized possession: the slingshot with which he and the boys had competed with such fervor over who could hit more accurately the spot on an electric pole where it should have been connected to something but wasn't.

Then they wheeled him around and led him into one of the houses where his portion of wedding pilau was waiting for him. Sticky opalescent rice to seal his fate. A fate not so different from the fate of most men in Oqa, scripted by centuries of life and war in the desert: he would draw murky water by rope out of an open well seventy-five feet deep. He would never have enough to eat, and his teenage wife would grow old by her second child. God willing, the children would live past the age of five. His wife would weave carpets and support his family. He would smoke opium to take his mind off his tribulations. He never would learn to read and write. His honeymoon would last three days, and then Ozyr Khul would return to collecting calligonum thorns under agonizing sun to barter in Zadyan or Khairabad or Karaghuzhlah for oil and rice and wheat.

"The boy is very young," said Amanullah. "He won't know what to do with the bride. He may just end up smelling her, that's all."

"Nowadays, they grow up so quickly," replied Janni the warlord. "I'm sure he knows everything there's to know already."

And that was the last time anyone ever would make any jokes about Ozyr Khul's age or male prowess. After all, the whole village and the whole desert and really the whole world were complicit in his marriage. It was they who had decided that it was time for the boy to become a man.

The forward-moving rhythm of the women's songs egged the sun up, up, up into the sky, and on, on, on across the flat world until the wedding day turned into the wedding night. Across the tiny and at once immense world where Ozyr Khul now was the head of a household and Naim at last was no longer a bachelor. Then a fast and technicolor sunset flashed over the village, and it was dark, and the epicanthic moon rose out of the eastern haze to blot out the Big Dipper star by star.

〜〜〜

A few days after the wedding, after most of the guests had gone back to their own villages and towns and the west wind had caked with a film of fine golden moon dust the large home-stitched triangular amulets that hung above the doors of the two newlywed couples to protect their marriages from the evil eye, Thawra returned to her loom room with a chipped glass cup of hot green tea in one hand and the green thermos with three fading tulips in the other.

She leaned over the loom and set the cup in an alcove next to a pair of her husband's black rubber shoes shaped like sneakers and turned the cup so that its handle faced the room. She placed the thermos on the floor. She straightened up and, as she did each time before setting to work, adjusted her headscarf where it tied at the nape. She shook off her rubber flip-flops—*thwack, thwack*—and stepped in bare feet upon the foot-long section of the rug she had already woven. The tight and springy pile of the world's most beautiful carpet pushed against the callus of her indigent soles.

The woman squatted facing north. She glanced at the unfinished design of her handiwork, the flowers unbloomed, the lines uncrossed. Then she picked up the end of an indigo thread and ran it around two warps and pulled on it and cut it off with a sickle.

Thk.

In the bedroom across the hallway, Baba Nazar, Amanullah, and Nurullah slouched together on a mattress, half asleep. On the *namad* in front of them stood the old transistor radio that had blared

Turkoman songs during the first wedding in Oqa in a decade. Now it was crackling war news. In the province of Helmand, said the radio, NATO troops fired from the air on two houses raised with clay and straw, just like Baba Nazar's own house. The air strike killed twelve children and two women . . . In the city of Taloqan, at the eastern end of the barchan belt that stretched past Oqa, a Taliban suicide bomber killed an important mujaheddin commander who had supervised all Afghan security forces north of the Hindu Kush. Several other people, Afghan and German, died in the explosion . . . American troops near the city of Jalalabad stormed a compound of a sleeping family and killed a twelve-year-old girl and her uncle, a married man who had two little girls of his own. NATO said the soldiers had raided the wrong house and apologized for the mistake . . . A suicide bomber blew up in a tent at a hospital in Kabul where medical students were eating a poor man's lunch of rice and tea. There were many dead . . . Four Taliban gunmen stormed and held for ten bloody hours a government building in the city of Khost. There were many dead . . . A roadside bomb ripped through a truck that was carrying two score penniless day laborers to dredge irrigation canals somewhere in Kandahar. There were many dead . . .

Thawra reached for her teacup and took four loud sips and tossed the dregs at the wall. Amber drops and tea leaves trickled down the unfired clay and splashed at the pale wefts and in less than a minute all the liquid was absorbed completely. Only a light yellow stain on the yarn remained, barely noticeable among splotches of chicken shit and dust and bits of straw that had stuck to the thread. *Thk, thk, thk,* Thawra's sickle counted out the hours to the next disaster.

After a while, Boston entered the loom room with her own tea in a porcelain *piala* and sat down on the floor next to the carpet to rest. Her rest lasted as long as it took her to sip her tea once. Then, with a loud sigh and a crack of arthritic bones, she rose and took off her own slippers. Her feet were gorgeous, narrow, finely veined, the color of the sand dunes outside. She squatted on the carpet next to Thawra and picked up a white thread.

It was quiet at the loom. The women worked fast and spoke little, in monosyllabic undertones. Near the northern beam, above the wefts she had strung herself at winter's end, little Leila was taking a nap in a small hammock her grandmother had woven with coarse saddlebag wool. You could hear her short shallow breaths, dreams escaping through a mouth half open. You could hear Boston's necklace of keys jingle from time to time, when the old woman leaned forward to peek through the two doorways that separated the women from the men and smile her quick schoolgirl smile, the smile of a heart at peace.

Two young roosters started a fight in the room. They circled each other, and then stood and stared for a long time, necks outstretched, then attacked, flying up, vicious, feathers and down spraying everywhere. Tiny dust puffs exploded from the floor. "Shoo!" Boston hissed at the roosters and they ignored her.

Two young girls walked in, Hazar Gul and a friend. They were wearing eye shadow, uneven strokes of metallic blue and sunset orange. Their mouths were dirty at the corners, their cheeks smeared with grime, their hair cropped short for the summer and stiff with dust. They were extraordinarily pretty. Two runaway starlets. They were chewing gum and their mastication was the loudest sound in the room. "Shoo!" Boston hissed again, and the girls ignored her as well.

"Look at this," a Mazar-e-Sharif carpet merchant told me once. His name was Jamshid Bigzada, and he was watching the shop for his older brother, Satar Bigzada, a broad and thunderous Uzbek who had a weak heart, six children, thinning gray hair, and—it said so on his business card—"All Kind Of All Carpet Khwaja Roshani Shereen Taqab Afghani Irani Ibrashimi Moori Available Here." Bigzada's shop occupied a section of the first floor of a glass-and-concrete hotel built catercorner from the Blue Mosque during the Communist rule. It faced a perpetual chaotic clot of *zaranj* motor-rickshaws and taxis and horse-drawn carts and motorbikes and bicycles. Legless beggars crawled through this tangle of human and beast and machine, and snotty barefoot boys darted in and out of traffic to thrust mangled cans smoldering with seeds of Syrian rue into the windows of motorists to protect them from curses and earn the boys a few coppers.

To enter the shop, you climbed four or five steps up from the paved stretch of sidewalk where an old man was selling whichever fruit were in season that week and another old man was selling dusty prayer beads and coins from the time of Alexander the Great and the time of the Raj and the time of Zahir Shah and the time of the Soviets. You removed your shoes at the concrete threshold worn to a silver sheen by generations of visitors. Silhouetting in the back-lit doorway, you placed your right hand on your heart in a gesture of humility and greeting and stepped inside.

Stepped into a Caravaggio painting. About four hundred carpets lay folded in shoulder-high stacks and hung from walls and draped low divans and lay on the floor one upon the other in a disorder that recalled waterline kelp. The wool suffused the room in burgundy twilight. A kind of regal semidarkness that made you want to bow, that hued everything inside a deeper and more profound shade, like an icon blackened by centuries of supplicants' candles. Sometimes a white dove, one of the ten thousand said to flock to the mosque, would flutter into the shop and perch on a rug, unearthly pale against the kidney wool, unabsorbable, breaking through all the intense cinnabar and carmine and cerise, and then everyone in the shop would point to it and nod meaningfully and agree that the bird was a good omen. And that in itself was fortunate because—here the merchants and their customers would invoke the witness of God—Afghanistan needed as many good omens as it could get.

"Look at this," repeated Jamshid, and pulled out from the middle of a pile of carpets and spread before me a *yusufi* much like the one Thawra was weaving in Oqa. "The women who weave are illiterate and very poor. But they make this unbelievable beauty."

Study your carpet. The hands of three generations of illiterate women created it. It is soiled by chicken droppings and stained yellow where the weaver threw her tea dregs at the loom. Its knots fasten wedding songs and women's murmurs. The metronome of a sickle blade and the buzzing of noon flies. The whistle of a gale in the grass roof. An old woman's breath as she, at last, sat down on the floor to rest.

The women wove their carpet of whispers. I leaned against the doorway and took notes.

A lizard skittered from underneath the loom and up a clay wall and disappeared. From time to time I would look up from my notebook to watch the women weave. From time to time they would look up from their loom to watch me scribble. Silently, discreetly, we studied one another. To each of us, the other's craft unknowable, full of mysteries.

Sometimes we would catch one another's eyes and laugh together without making a sound.

It was mid-afternoon, very hot. The whole village was quiet, stagnant. Everyone was either napping or weaving. No one was outside. The unpeopled landscape of Oqa was so sparse that each object stood out. Bed. Artillery shell casing. Donkey. Dung beetle. Tandoor. Time felt dilated, molten, distilled to its core: a wartime wedding feast for children. Armed nocturnal riders through a desert always on the cusp of bloodshed. Another spring at the loom.

THE FAST

~~~

T he desert flowed over the thin paved band of the Great Silk Road. It slipped, it grabbed on to the tiniest pebbles on the tarmac and built miniature barchans around each one, it cascaded down one gray billow of loess to climb upon the next—always moving, moving, moving, constant, persistent, hypnotic, weaving its own magic carpet ride over Turkestan, rising and falling, rising sometimes all the way to the ocher sky in airborne swirls, smearing the skyline with aurorae borealis of sand, murmuring the hoofbeat plainsongs of caravans of yore, the hourglass breath of the passage of time, the whispered hymns of passage.

Out of such sand issued four motorcycles. They bounced up and down a white unpaved track that approached the highway from the south and dragged behind them four individual mantels of pallid dancing dust. One motorcycle wobbled in front; the others advanced side by side a couple hundred yards farther back. Each carried two riders.

At the asphalt road the lead motorcycle rolled to a stop. A beat-up machine of some former color. Behind the wheel a sandaled man in a checkered turban and dun *shalwar kameez*. Behind him a woman in a blue burqa. She was sitting astride, and the pleats of her veil had bunched around her shins. You could see, beneath the nylon, the pure white openwork lace of the fringes of her panta-loons, the dark bony ankles, the scuffed narrow brown mules. The woman held on to the man's waist with one hand. Her other hand embraced a tall narrow bundle, taller than her head, that stood up-right on the seat between her legs: a carpet, furled pile side in.

Apart from the protean feathers of drifting sand, the highway was empty. The driver turned the steering wheel left and walked the motorcycle onto the blacktop and revved the hiccupping engine, and the carpet and its guardians clanked off along the ancient trade route westward, in the direction of the nearest big town, Andkhoi, the smuggling gateway on the border with Turkmenistan. The And-khoi bazaar was open for commerce that day, for it was Monday.

A heavy rumble came from the east. Up from a dry ravine climbed a convoy of six or seven enormous and faceless armored machines, futuristic to the point of being extraterrestrial, mutant insects from a science-fiction horror film, also traveling west. Some flew German flags. They overtook the motorcycle and dropped be-hind the next hill.

The rest of the motorcycles pulled up to the intersection. They did not slow down when they reached the asphalt. They banked right at elegant fifty-degree angles in unison and kept going. Their riders were men in camouflage and dark turbans. The drivers ap-peared unarmed. The passengers held on one-handed to the waists of the drivers. With their free hands, they gripped Kalashnikov ri-fles, which they had propped vertically on the seats between their thighs, upright on the guns' wooden butts, the muzzles taller than the riders' heads. They sped east, toward Mazar-e-Sharif, and soon disappeared into the ravine. Then only sand eddied along the pitch. One day some of these grains might shape the barchans of Oqa.

The Great Silk Road suffered all travelers, as it had done for centuries.

Once every few days, in the dim sanctum of their shop on Carpet Row, the Bigzada brothers of Mazar-e-Sharif rolled their wares into long and narrow plastic bags stamped with the English words "Afghan Carpet Exporter" and "Gift of the Carpet Association from Zone Shamal (Afghanistan)." These they dispatched in two general directions.

Many went south to Kabul in cargo holds of buses or in flatbeds of trucks. From the capital, some flew to Dubai and then onward, to London, Frankfurt, New York. The rest continued by truck east on the Grand Trunk Road, across the border to Pakistan, to the bazaars of Peshawar and Islamabad.

Others traveled on the Great Silk Road west toward Andkhoi, across the border with Turkmenistan, across the Karakum Desert, and onward to the markets of Istanbul, the world capital of carpet trade.

After squirming out of the earsplitting traffic jams of Mazar-e-Sharif, the road leveled out onto monochrome ashen plains. "Acred cerements," Robert Byron wrote of this land. Vastitudes of dark defeat. The road sped past Genghis Khan's slaughter fields of Balkh. It sliced through the blood-soaked expanse of Dasht-e-Leili, where skeletonweed flowers blinked above the unmarked mass graves of some two thousand Taliban prisoners of war. The Uzbek warlord Abdul Rashid Dostum, paid by the CIA to command his illiterate and half-starved army of mujaheddin and farmers and children—the ground troops of the United States' invasion—massacred these Taliban fighters here in 2001 in the first landmark atrocity in America's war on terror. The road ran past all the forgotten battlefields in between, past a stately camel caravan and past three boys who squatted in a line to urinate into a ditch. Past herds of fat-tailed sheep whose caudal appendages sometimes grew so large there were tales of shepherds having to hitch carts to the animals to support the weight of their fat. That fat, the seventeenth-century German orientalist Hiob Ludolf reported, was "a medium between tallow and butter, and an excellent substitute for lard . . . and by many preferred to butter, which, in hot weather, is apt to grow rancid." More camels, more sheep. The Great Silk Road dragged its backdrop along with it across the desert and across centuries like a traveling circus trundling along with its illusory and faded mise-en-scène that was bequeathed down generations and reused over and over.

In Andkhoi the road slowed down to curl around the main town square, named after Mir Alisher Nava'i: Afghan statesman, scholar, poet, patron of the arts and sciences, the father of Turkic literature. Nava'i had lived farther south on the Great Silk Road, in lush and blue-tiled Herat, in the fifteenth century, but he had traveled the road to Balkh at least once, to solve a diplomatic dispute between the Herati emir—the poet's foster brother and employer—and his rebellious son. "Let me learn by paradox . . . / that the valley is the place of vision," Nava'i wrote. Which visions did Andkhoi offer a passing traveler, besides the echoes of the olden journeys of others? A lethargic oasis on an ancient caravan route, a dull two-story outpost that some said had been founded by Alexander the Great. Almost

treeless, besieged-looking, perpetually umber from frequent sandstorms. "Grey earth, grey camels, grey walls and cubic houses," the Swiss journalist Ella K. Maillart described the Andkhoi she saw in 1939, when she and Annemarie Schwarzenbach drove through in their Ford. But it was in one of these gray cubes on a cold winter night that I was mothered by a kind woman only two years my senior who pinched my cheek and then kissed her fingertips, who heated water for my bucket shower and made room for me under the heavy blanket she already shared with five of her children, a teenage niece, and a coal stove; and the walls of the room swayed to our communal breath, and the visions I had were of a family that I knew, in that twilight state under Karima's blanket, I could be part of if only I could resist the diaphragmatic tug of the Great Silk Road, or of a road, any road at all.

The road curled around Nava'i Square. Past the squat whitewashed mosque that also bore the poet's name ("Lord, in the daytime stars can be seen from the deepest wells, / and the deeper the wells the brighter thy stars shine"). Past the cross-legged traders who worried their prayer beads at stalls that sold hand-embroidered dresses and aluminum serving platters and karakul lambskins and rosewater-scented soap labeled "Spacial Soup," and in shops where restless iridescent flies buzzed and electric lights went on and off, on and off, even more restless than the flies. The men bemoaned the rising price of wool, the unreliable electricity, the daylight kidnappings at checkpoints set up by who knows whom, the suicide bombings that were becoming frequent.

"Life is poor dirt."

"The price of carpets isn't worth the trouble."

"During the day, they attack travelers, merchants carrying goods to market."

"But overall, security is okay. The government is here during the day, and at night we have the Taliban."

The road trawled through the square thick with the merchants' laments and then straightened out again and sped up, jutting northwest toward Aqina, the Turkmen border crossing.

I followed the carpet route to that border twice. Both times a haboob blew.

Afghans call such storms *tufan*. They begin with an eldritch noontime dusk, a buttermilk fog of steaming dust that devours horizons and flaps the tattered streamers on roadside graves like signal flags of distress and turns inside out the silver leaves of poplar trees that grow by the curbs in occasional square groves, to be cut down for roof beams. Then comes an enormous bruise-colored roller of sand, taller than the scarps of the hillocks where magpies nest in narrow hollows, taller than the mountains wrinkled with millennial sheep paths, taller than the sky itself. Then comes a nothingness, a sepia vacuum, a sudden blindness.

Qaqa Satar rolled the car to a stop where he thought the asphalt ended and the desert began, and we waited. Minutes passed. Maybe half an hour. Then we began to see, first the hood of his dilapidated Toyota, then the outline of the road immediately in front. The air remained yellow and muddy, like tea in Oqa. Qaqa Satar turned the ignition key and started west again, slowly. We passed oil tankers with Turkish writing. We passed a truck that implored in red English script: HOW IS MY DRIVING? We passed motor-rickshaws that had names: Tiger Zarang. Corzun Asli. Zarang. Almas Hashemi. Armed riders, carpet weavers, NATO invaders, smugglers, merchants, the *tufan*—ultimately they were all the same, all knots in the old rug of the Khorasan.

At the border. A wave train of chain-link fences growing out of the sand and receding into it. Like fishing nets abandoned at low tide by prehistoric fishermen in a vanished antediluvian sea. A grubby bazaar selling Chinese blankets and over-the-counter Korean cigarettes and under-the-counter vodka from Uzbekistan, fiery and vile. Pools of motor oil underfoot. A bored chief of customs with Brezhnev eyebrows and hair dyed blueblack behind a polished, palm-size chunk of lapis lazuli shaped like the map of Afghanistan with his name engraved in it. Border guards outside, hands perpetually extended for a handshake, a cigarette, a bribe.

I was following two men in dirty two-piece suits and plastic flip-flops. The men were carrying toward the border crossing a carpet, or carpets, rolled up into a burlap sack. They carried the sack the way two men might carry a corpse. Each man holding one end of the bundle. Taking tiny sandaled steps toward the coveted gate in the mesh fence. They showed some papers to a border guard, handed him a wad of banknotes, and he let them pass. I had no papers to approach the gate, so I was held up. A small uniformed crowd formed. At last, one of the border guards announced: "No problem. She's not Pakistani. She won't blow herself up on the border. She can go."

Each week, Brezhnev Eyebrows informed me, several hundred carpets left Afghanistan through this border. Each week two hundred trucks entered the country carrying petrol, cigarettes, candy, shoes, toys, clothes, cell phones, booze.

By the time I reached the gate beyond which Turkmenistan lay, the men were gone from sight. And I could go no farther: I had no visa to enter Turkmenistan. I squinted to keep the dust out of my eyes. Beyond this frontier Amanullah had imagined beautiful girls who were waiting to lavish upon him their nightingale songs, their exquisite caresses. Had he come with me to Aqina, he would have been heartbroken. On the other side of the sea of fences there were no girls at all. A few eighteen-wheelers waited for clearance and dripped motor oil, and that was it. And the unbounded Karakum Desert crept steadily westward, blurring earth and sky. Its name meant "black sand," but it was not black. It was the pallid color of a tombstone. It made my throat dry. It made my head spin. I saw more than two thousand years of thirsty caravans winding their improbable way through that rimless, heartless waste.

My companion, a young Mazari man who had come on the trip with me to translate, saw something else entirely.

"I want to go across," he whispered, in English.

"What would you do there?"

"Nightclubs. I miss nightclubs."

"Have you even been to a nightclub?"

"No." There were no nightclubs in Mazar-e-Sharif.

"Then how can you miss them?"

"I saw it in film."

〜〜〜

At two in the morning the women of my house in Mazar-e-Sharif rose without a sound from tick mattresses sweet with sleep and lovemaking and children's breath and inexpressible loneliness. Quietly they stepped out of their bedrooms, pulled shut their doors, pulled tight their scarves over their bare shoulders, filed through the hallways hushed with cheap carpets woven by machines in some nameless Chinese factory, and entered the large second-floor kitchen. The city had power that night. The single fluorescent ceiling light went on.

Eight brothers lived in the house with their widowed mother—a kind and vulgar matriarch who had given birth nineteen times and had lost seven children in infancy, and who commanded the house with unflinching and unquestioned authority despite debilitating joint pain, high blood pressure, and silent and devastating lovesickness for her dead husband—and their hardworking youngest sister, who was said to have a temper and therefore, already in her early twenties, remained single. Four of the brothers were married and their wives lived with them; three had children of their own. Most of the year, the two-story poured-concrete house reverberated with a near-constant ruckus of screaming infants, quarreling toddlers, singing teenagers, jokes, chaffs, marital arguments, orders bellowed from one end of the compound to another, counterorders shrilled back, dishes clanging, doors slamming, the slapping of wet laundry against an aluminum basin, the whacking of a butcher knife against a wooden chopping board, the bounce-bounce-bouncing of a soccer ball on the cement floor of the yard, on the carpeting of the hallways, the cymballic syncopations of Bollywood tunes on the radio—often different tunes in several rooms at once.

Outside, a film of violence and death swirled and pooled over the province of Balkh like the rainbow plumes of an oil slick. During the ten weeks that had passed since Ozyr Khul and Naim had taken each other's sisters as wives, farmers had clustered into armed gangs and clashed with Taliban fighters. The Taliban had shot dead a teacher from Siogert who had urged fellow villagers to resist the militia's demand for tithes. Someone had fired rocket-propelled grenades into the compound of an elder in Shahrak, twice; both grenades had missed the house and bit into the cracked clay ground and exploded in black balloons of burnt dust. Four people died during a cholera outbreak in Dawlatabad. Six blocks south of my noisy house in Mazar, a bicyclist had detonated a bomb and killed three children and the grocer my hosts had known as the Old Man on the Corner. Men who said they were Taliban had telephoned one of the brothers in my house several times. They said they would kill him because he had helped the police identify and arrest one of the men who had led the attack that spring on the United Nations office in Mazar-e-Sharif, where my host worked as a driver. They said they would gouge out his eyes. They said they would track down his children and kidnap them. Night watchmen's whistles in the city sounded more urgent, more dire.

Yet somehow the bloodshed and fear of that summer seemed only lightly traced upon the fixed topography of the land, the scarring of these latest war crimes and threats impermanent like drifting sand upon the immutable canvas of the plains and mountains, ready to be erased and rewritten anew the next summer, and the next, and the next. For the most part, life went on as it had forever. My Mazari hosts still smoked their mint-flavored waterpipe on starry Friday evenings. Village kids still played in irrigation ditches that sometimes oozed with warm mud. In Khairabad, men still sat on their haunches by wells and stared darkly down the road. In Karaghuzhlah, women still dried the bitter harvest of almonds on the clay stoops of their compounds. In Oqa, Thawra still wove her carpet, now almost two meters long.

And then, on the first night of August, a thread-thin new moon stitched through the sky and instantly sealed off all the pandemonium behind its arced parenthesis. Overnight the very internal landscape of the Khorasan became rearranged, adjusted to accommodate a rigid set of distinct and ancient rituals. The ninth lunar month of the Muslim calendar, the holy month of Ramadan, had begun.

Such tenderness reigned in the kitchen. The women worked in silence. Only when they passed one another coursing around the floor did they touch hands lightly and say one another's names and suffix them with an endearment. "Manija *jan.*" "Nilufar *jan.*" "Ruwaida *jan.*" On a two-burner gas stove they heated up leftover okra sauce and rice in a big cast-iron pot. The eldest of the wives, Nadia—"Nadia *jan*"—cooked a quick *lobio* of red beans. I chopped tomatoes and cucumbers and white onions into several small salad bowls and swept the floor with a balding broom. "Anna *jan*." No other words were uttered. Kotzia *jan*, the unmarried sister, at quarter to three spread a maroon plastic *dastarkhan* in the hallway, and the rest of us brought out teacups and long glass platters of beans and rice and okra and yesterday's nan stacked into a short pyramid and two thermoses of hot tea brewed the night before and a tray of sliced watermelon. We touched hands. We smiled. The matriarch made her way heavily upstairs and sat on the carpet and leaned against the wall and moaned quietly through her pain the name of God:

"Lordy, lordy."

She looked up.

"Sit, Anna *jan*." She patted the floor next to her. I hesitated. She grabbed my thigh and forced me down. "Sit, daughter. Sit here next to me."

Her name was Qalam Nissa. No one called her that. She was *Madar*—Mother—or *Madar jan*—dear Mother. Dear Mother the sorceress, who would throw water from a red pitcher after me when I would leave the house, to protect me from the evil of the road. Dear Mother the bonesetter, who, after I had fallen off a horse, tried to fix my wrist and laughed when I screamed louder than I had thought possible. Who would come into my room to drink tea and mourn her husband's death of blood cancer and check that I was warm enough, cool enough, fed enough, loved enough, and, one evening, to squeeze my breasts with both stubby hands and demand: "How come your tits are so small? Look at mine!"

Her chest was colossal, like her love.

Dear Mother the midwife, who had grown up illiterate in a mountain village in eastern Afghanistan and had delivered more babies than she could remember, including those of her two married daughters and of her sons' wives, and thereby—in her mind at least—had earned the right to offer, in the kitchen while her daughters-in-law and I did the cooking, a comparative analysis of the women's physiology.

"My cunt is like this," she explained in Farsi, and drew her fingers into a tight fist. "Ruwaida's cunt is like this," and she loosened the fist and flapped her wrist up and down, like a dog's tongue. "Nilufar's is like this—*waah, waah!*" and her fingers became a hungry bird crying for food. She looked at me and grinned.

"And your cunt, Anna?"

"Enough already, Mother!" shouted one of the women. Everyone else was squealing with laughter.

"Shush, girl—and your cunt, Anna? What's your cunt like? You have one, don't you?"

And she reached out and pinched my crotch, and I blushed. I could never keep up, in any language.

Of course, in kitchens all over Afghanistan, women traded sex jokes, often in two-line verse.

> *I will gladly give you my mouth,*
> *But why stir my pitcher? Here I am now, all wet—*

went these *landays*, unrhymed and proverbial, bitter and teasing, composed in Pashto and repeated over decades, over centuries. They had no one author but belonged to everywoman, and so she threw them into vats of pilau along with pinches of cumin—

> *Is there not a single madman in this village?*
> *My pants, the hue of fire, are burning on my thighs—*

and kneaded them into the air bubbles that sneaked inside the ragged loaves of nan, and wove them into carpets—

> *My love, jump into bed with me and do not fear,*
> *If it should break the "little horror" is there for the repair.*

Landay, the Pashto word for a short snake full of venom. The "little horror," explained the Afghan poet and *landay* collector Sayd Bahodine Majrouh, was the husband, the "companion . . . forced upon her"—often an old man, like Zarifshah Bibi's husband, Mustafa, or a child, like Ozyr Khul.

But during the first Ramadan breakfast, Qalam Nissa was quiet, groggy with sleep, hushed by the solemnity of the occasion, awed by the twenty-nine impending days of thirst and hunger. All she said to me was, "Sit with me, daughter."

And I sat.

I once asked Qalam Nissa what, as a little girl in a village of stone homes and emerald brooks, she had wanted to become when she grew up.

"A mother," she said. "I wanted to become a mother. And here I am."

· · ·

We sat. Qalam Nissa's sons came out of the bedrooms in their tank tops and wrinkled pantaloons, tiptoed to the *dastarkhan*, sat. Their wives sat. Their unmarried sister, Kotzia, sat. We ate little. We spoke in whispers. Only adults fasted for Ramadan, and the children were asleep. The house was never this quiet at mealtime. For the last forty minutes of this nocturnal breakfast, we drank and drank tea until "the white thread of dawn appear . . . distinct from its black thread," as prescribed in The Heifer, the second sura of the Koran. And then, just after four o'clock, the call to prayer sounded, and the family wiped their lips for the day. The men put on their knee-length shirts and went to the mosque, and the women finished cleaning up and went back to sleep. The next time anyone would eat or drink would be after seven at night, after the sun had subdued and then flashed one last burst of violent crimson over the western desert, and the mare's tails over the Hindu Kush to the south had lit up purple and burgundy and faded to inky black, and Venus had risen large as a ping-pong ball in the eastern sky, and the thirsty voices of the muezzins, amplified by a hundred crackly megaphones, had told the city that the first day of the fast was over.

~~~~

That morning I walked out of the compound in Mazar-e-Sharif into a grid of blinding unpaved streets.

It was nine o'clock. At eight, four hours after the predawn meal and three hours later than usual in summer, the men of the house had gone to work in the city, and the women had stirred out of their rooms to feed the children, then retreated to their unmade beds. Qalam Nissa, in her nightclothes, peeked out of her bedroom to ask me where I was going—*"Shahr,"* I said, "downtown"—and she wished me to go with God and moved her hand as if to bless me but then, overcome by fatigue, shut her door and went back to sleep. All the curtains in the house were drawn and would remain so until the month was over.

The white sun of August had veiled the Hindu Kush with stagnant haze and flattened the Khorasan into a two-dimensional eggshell pancake. It had blanched thistle plants down to translucent rattling husks among which sheep and goats kept their heads tucked low into the stark blue pools of their own shadows. Humans squatted against clay walls that threw miserly slivers of shade. Excruciating days were spent waiting for the slightly cooler nights, when it was thinkable to unfold, to stretch, to stand tall again. When it was possible, at last, to drink.

I moved at a crawl. So did everything else. The few cars that were out. The occasional horse-drawn cart. The rare pedestrians—men in clean *shalwar kameez*, women in burqas or in the white Ramadan headscarves of chastity, of schoolgirls—crept down the streets, clinging to the rope-thin strips of shadow that hemmed bone-white walls. Even the sunlit dust that, stirred by passing trucks, rose from the potholes in a slow pink motion hesitated to billow and then hung above the road long after the trucks had gone. Ramadan decelerated all movement, congealed time, rang in the ears with the white noise of thirst, like the aura of an approaching migraine.

On Dasht-e-Shor Street, which bounced south from my neighborhood toward the Blue Mosque, most shops were shuttered. The shopkeepers in the stores that did stay open were lying on their backs on clammy carpets or charpoy rope beds in the thin light that seeped through half-open doors, trying to expend as little energy as possible and not to sweat the precious liquids. There were no customers. No one spoke except to wish one another a peaceful Ramadan: to open your lips was to dry out your tongue, and then how to survive the ten hours till iftar? An intolerable hush sifted through the city. Women who gathered to fast together stopped talking one by one after a few minutes of lament, pointing with their forefingers at their mouths, and then sat fanning themselves with the fringes of their scarves in dehydrated silence. The sorriest were the child vendors who stood under improbable awnings of ripped canvas beside large plastic coolers full of individual packets of pomegranate and cherry juice, the packets soggy from the melting ice and no longer very cold. Little old men with crow's-feet of disillusionment and suspicion around their dull and exhausted eyes, underage breadwinners who worked in the stalls of their fathers, their uncles, their widowed mothers. Who would buy their juice at this hour? Even those who did not observe the fast—the travelers, the sick, the pregnant or menstruating women, the lackadaisical Muslims—would have been ashamed to drink in public.

And it was hot, hot, unforgivably hot. I lasted two hours on my walk. Then I went home and shut the door to my bedroom to read Rumi.

> *Be emptier and cry like reed instruments cry.*
> *Emptier, write secrets with the reed pen.*
> *When you're full of food and drink, an ugly metal*
> *statue sits where your spirit should. When you fast,*
> *good habits gather like friends who want to help.*
> *Fasting is Solomon's ring.*

Perhaps so. I was very thirsty. I prayed a heathen's prayer for the night to come.

At four in the afternoon the women of the house emerged from their rooms again to get going on the iftar dinner.

Iftar in Qalam Nissa's house, invariably, was *bolani*, the savory, deep-fried stuffed pancakes made fresh each night. Sometimes the women would serve *dogh*, the salty drink of diluted yogurt and garlic; dates, which the Prophet Mohammed had eaten to break his own fast; and lemonade made with powder imported from Iran. Occasionally someone would prepare rice or veal pilau, and once I dared to cook a large vat of chicken curry, which the family said was good but a little too spicy.

(The grainy rice I had made to accompany the curry was rejected. It was not sticky, and difficult to eat by hand. My hosts unanimously agreed that it was undercooked. "Do you feed this to your children?" one of the brothers asked. "Is it even safe?" And, when I blushed in embarrassment, he offered this comfort: "You should watch our women sometimes. They will teach you to make rice properly.")

But *bolani* were a Ramadan staple in Northern Afghanistan. In my house they were prepared collectively on a large tarp covered by a clean white bedsheet and spread on the hallway floor next to the kitchen. One of the women kneaded the dough and shaped it into balls the size of a fist; two rolled the balls into thin round crepes; the rest arranged the stuffing on them, folded them in half, pinched the sides together. The ritual was the same in every city household, though the number of cooks varied. Each afternoon thousands of thirsty and sweltering women knelt on the floors of their kitchens and hallways in an inadvertent unison, a city-scale ballet of flour puffs. The wife and teenage daughter of Satar Bigzada, sweating, smiling, joking in whispered Uzbek. The mother and sisters of the young Hazara woman who worked as my translator that month. Qalam Nissa's two married daughters and their own teenage girls. The wife and daughters of her oldest son who lived separately, four blocks away. Qaqa Satar's wife.

And then the families would sit together around the oily golden piles and fan themselves and wait for that magical moment of gloaming when the city would hang suspended from a double layer of lace: of holiday prayer streaming horizontally from a hundred crepitating loudspeakers, and of old light streaming down from myriad stars.

"Bolani," said Amanullah, and closed his eyes, and imagined the bubbling half-moons of deep-fried dough, the delicate, thinly lay-

ered stuffing of minced garlic greens, or of pureed potatoes, or of crushed pumpkin, or maybe even—delicious, unbelievable—of spiced sheep tripe. Imagined folding these pies in half with burning fingers and dipping them in cool fresh yogurt. Imagined the way they must crunch and melt in his perpetually hungry mouth.

He smiled, eyes still shut.

"Would be nice."

⌇⌇⌇

Once upon a time the moon was white, and the sun and the moon had a fight over who was more beautiful. The sun said it was more beautiful because its beauty illuminated the entire world. The moon said it was more beautiful because its face was completely white. Then the sun got angry and collected desert sand, dust, and the ashes from its *bukhari* and threw them at the moon. The dirt soiled the moon's face forever. The moon became embarrassed and stopped coming out during the day. That's why the moon comes only at night and its face is blemished."

Finished with the story, Amanullah wiped his forehead with the loose end of his turban, and in an instant his skin was beaded with sweat again. It was very hot in his cob house. Outside it was hotter still. Weather forecasts showed the mercury at one hundred and twenty degrees Fahrenheit, dipping to one hundred at night. The desert throbbed in the dry heat. Amanullah squinted at the cigarette he was holding between his thumb and forefinger to gauge whether there was any more tobacco left in it worth smoking and took one last drag and tossed the squashy butt in the direction of the door.

He could not recall the last time he had eaten *bolani*. Few people in Oqa could. *Bolani* were a rich-man's food. Who in the village could bear the exorbitant expense of the stuffing—of pumpkins, of heart-red tomatoes, of the piquant jade bouquets of garlic shoots that sweated tangy green juice where they were bruised by the butcher's string that bunched them together? Not to mention how much precious oil was required to deep-fry the pancakes. My hosts in Mazar would use half a liter just to cook each night's batch.

"The oil we use for cooking—what's it made out of?" Amanullah asked once. We were sitting on the *namad* with his daughter, Leila, who had squirreled a handful of sunflower seeds between her thighs and was plucking them one by one delicately with her thumb and forefinger and shucking them with her teeth. Amanullah reached under her legs to pilfer her batch, but she squeezed her thighs together and corkscrewed her bony buttocks deeper into the felt rug to stop her father's hand. He always was trying to filch her snacks—candy, a piece of chewing gum. She always was possessive of them. All toddlers are.

I pointed to Leila's seeds.

"Probably sunflower."

"I doubt it. We could never make as much oil as we use out of sunflowers."

Amanullah closed his eyes and took a quick imaginary journey around the rectangular carpet-world. "I think there is some animal in the river or the mountains that they kill and make oil out of."

In his landlocked hamlet, Amanullah envisioned Moby-Dick.

Then again, the iftar *bolani* carried little significance in the empty bowl of Oqa. Like the paroxysms of cyclical violence that concussed the Khorasan, or the twenty-first-century infrastructural advancements that veneered parts of Afghanistan's largest cities, Ramadan seemed to reach Oqa only in echo. The silver stroke of the shamefaced moon over the desert that month announced to the villagers no holy observance.

"Here in Oqa there is no fast," said Amin Bai, and chewed his cigarette butt over to the corner of his mouth.

"Why not?"

The Commander smiled. His beige skullcap was dark with sweat.

"Why keep fast in this heat?"

And Baba Nazar added with the special patience one reserves for explaining simple truths to an obtuse child: "Look at us. Here in Oqa we fast every day of the year."

He had taken his shotgun to the dunes twice that week, and twice he had come home empty-handed. Not even a rabbit for Boston to cook into a dark cottony stew. Each year the barren land around the village became more barren, he said—for want of water, maybe, or maybe because all the animals had been hunted and eaten. The spindly-legged gray chickens that had hatched upon Thawra's carpet in July were still too small to eat. For days the family's only sustenance was homemade bread and foamy camel yogurt and the almonds Boston would shuck with a large rusty pestle on the piece of tarp Amanullah had used that winter to roof Thawra's loom room, and tea. In the house of Choreh and Choreh Gul the *dastarkhan* was emptier still—tea one day, bread the next, no almonds. Opium to take care of the hunger pangs. Baby Zakrullah had developed a respiratory infection, and his mother was too stoned to wipe the crust of green mucus off his upper lip. Only Hazar Gul remained buoyant through the hunger and the heat, and spent long hours in the half-light of Thawra's loom room, squatting on top of the carpet, weaving sometimes, always smiling.

And in the loom room, which Amanullah had shielded from the hard sun with fresh armloads of dusty thistle, Thawra was running out of tan thread, the thread that made up the background for her carpet's stylized flowers and trees and eagles, the thread that tied into the most knots.

"We need a kilo more," Baba Nazar said. That was almost four dollars he had to produce—from where? "One meter is left. Winter is coming, we don't know whether she'll be weaving then. Maybe it will take her a month to finish. Maybe she'll have a baby in a month."

Thawra squatted upon the loom. Her calico dress hung off her thin shoulders and bulged very slightly around the compact swelling of her pregnancy. Behind her, the recently hatched chickens loped upon the tan weave between discarded candy wrappers and long-bladed scissors, and clucked. Baba Nazar leaned against the doorless entryway and clucked also, with worry. His eyes watered past the chickens and past his daughter-in-law, past even the striations of the room's hand-slapped walls, fixed on the invisible boundaries of his village's paucity.

Amanullah had his own reasons for not observing the fast. They were vintage Amanullah.

"Fasting and prayer are for old people," he announced. "I'm

young, so I don't fast and I don't pray. I'll start when I know that I'm going to die soon. Pray and fast later, when you're old and stay in the house all day. When you're young, you should enjoy life, you are so full of strength."

And to illustrate his point, he went on to explain how a friend who had traveled all the way to Kabul and back had brought him a special blue rhomboid pill that allowed him to keep an erection for more than thirty minutes and how with that erection he, Amanullah, had sex with Thawra until she begged him to stop, and how he would like to get his hands on another one of those special blue pills.

"Would be nice," he repeated.

And added, on the subject of fasting: "I heard it says in the Koran that we shouldn't hurt ourselves. So I'm not hurting myself."

In fact, the Koran says the following: "Allah intends every facility for you; He does not want to put you to difficulties." Even Archangel Gabriel, in the almost twenty-three years he had spent dictating verbatim the word of God to the Prophet Mohammed, must have forgotten to consider the privations of Oqa.

❯❯❯

That Ramadan, the water in Oqa's wells dropped three feet.

"Oy, Khoda *jan*," the villagers would sough God's name after they leaned over the southern well and lowered the yellow plastic ten-liter bucket into the double girdle of concrete well rings on a frayed twisted rope of manila hemp. The bucket once had held cooking oil. It took longer to fall, and it took the villagers three more hand-over-hand heaves to haul the full bucket back up. Then they would pour the water into one of their own yellow jerry cans that still sometimes bore fading and shredded labels with the names of the products they once had contained—motor oil, cooking oil, paint thinner—and lower the bucket into the well again and bring it up again, each time invoking the name of God, seventy-eight feet of cordage burning their palms instead of seventy-five, until their yellow fleet of plastic containers was full of brackish and murky water, and it was time to lug them all the way up the cracked earth of the southern slope of their hummock.

The drought parched the entire Turkestan Plains. It shriveled and dried the harvest of almonds inside their porous hulls, and it withered apricot orchards spectral. It evaporated the tepid ooze from irrigation canals and sent *shamals* whispering through the dikes. It pulverized rice paddies into an ocher shroud that the hot wind of August picked up and hung between the land and the sky. Meteorologists in Europe were reporting that Afghanistan was in the fiftieth year of a continuous decline in rainfall.

In winter and early spring, the rain would linger, frozen, atop the bluest peaks of Bamyan until the warm months, when it would drip-feed Bactria's north-flowing Balkh River, which, in turn, would irrigate the thirsty fields and pastures through an elaborate and age-old tapestry of surface and underground ditches. But the volume of the water that drained each year into the turquoise head-waters of the Balkh River in Bamyan and gurgled, muddy with al-luvium, past the sonorous caverns of the Alborz Gorge and the hot springs of Chishmish Afa and there split off into manmade canals that distributed water throughout the province had shrunk almost by two-thirds over half a century. The meteorologists were predicting that within Amanullah's and Thawra's lifetimes a steady, unbroken drought would replace cyclical dry spells in Afghanistan for good.

How deep would the weaver and her husband need to lower the yellow plastic bucket into the diseased well then?

An engineer in Mazar-e-Sharif once drew for me a map of Balkh's irrigation system on a sheet of letter paper. He drew the map upside down, orienting it toward the south, the way he had been seeing it for twenty-five years out of the south-facing window of his office at the Northern River Basin Office of the Balkh Province Department of Water. The way he would have seen it that day had it not been for the sand that veiled completely the crags of the Hindu Kush, less than ten miles away, and almost everything in front of them as well.

In the top right corner the engineer drew some zigzags.

"Mountains," he said. "Bamyan."

He looked at me to check that I was following and then staccatoed the corner with a rash of dots.

"Snow."

A line sashayed through the dots and the zigzags.

"The Balkh River."

Two sets of contour lines on either side of the river, downstream.

"The Alborz Gorge. Chishmish Afa."

From there, the line split up into new lines that meandered north, toward the bottom of the page, and east. The engineer doubled some lines, wrote the names of the canals next to some others; he bit his lip in his effort, consumed entirely by the map, by the dikes that were running dry as he drew.

"To Mazar-e-Sharif." The engineer pointed at the canals on the paper. "To Balkh. To Shor Teppeh. To Dawlatabad. To Karaghuzhlah and Khairabad."

At Khairabad the line ended.

"To Oqa?" I asked, and pointed at the tip.

"To Oqa?" the engineer repeated. He held the pen halfway over the page. He frowned. "No. What's Oqa?"

～～～

A lone warplane circled low over the village. Boston and the men who had gathered to drink her tea in disregard of Ramadan followed its cold glint with their eyes.

"That plane is here to get Karim Jendi," Amanullah said. Everybody chuckled. Oqa was so far away from everything, so abandoned, so anonymous, so accidentally mapped at the lip of a barchan belt by some deranged cartographer, and Karim Jendi, a poor goatherd from Khairabad, was so insignificant and bedraggled a man, that the idea that the Americans would send a whole plane after him to this forlorn village did seem like a joke.

But privately, the men were worried. They knew from the newscasts that hissed through the speakers of Baba Nazar's radio that things like that happened. A jealous neighbor would report a man next door as an insurgent, and it would rain bombs. An irate creditor would say a defaulted sharecropper was a guerrilla commander, and soldiers would storm a sleeping compound at night with flash-bang grenades. And while there was no place to land a plane near the village, it would have been no surprise, in fact, if Americans had come to Oqa for Karim Jendi because the man who was after him had told the police that the goatherd was a dangerous Talib.

That man's name was Khan Geldi. He was a wealthy landlord who owned many acres of irrigated farmland and grazing fields in Khairabad and a house in Mazar-e-Sharif, in a neighborhood, just a few blocks from the Blue Mosque, where grape and bougainvillea vines climbed horizontal trellises to shade the neat tiles of secluded courtyards and where residents parked their absurdly clean Japanese cars alongside gutters that were almost never clogged with refuse. Under the Communists, Khan Geldi and his brother Rakhmon had served as Khalq administrators in Khairabad. Now they acted as elders for the village Turkomans. When someone had a family argument, they would separate the man from his wife. When someone had a land dispute, they would decide it.

The rich brothers exerted fairy-tale authority over their tribesmen, and their tribesmen ascribed to them fairy-tale flaws.

"They abuse the weak and steal from the indigent," said Baba Nazar.

"They take land from the poor people and say it belongs to them," said Amanullah.

"They wanted to take Karim Jendi's land, but he refused to give it to them," said Amin Bai.

After the final harvest of the previous fall, someone shot Rakhmon dead in a field outside Khairabad. Khan Geldi accused Karim Jendi of murdering his brother and told the police that Karim Jendi was an insurgent.

The police came to Khairabad for Karim Jendi four times. One time they brought with them foreign soldiers in two tanks. The foreigners parked their tanks in the cracked sun-fired pottery of the street where Karim Jendi's house stood and waited while the police searched the house for the goatherd but found only women and children. Another time the police came without foreigners and found Karim Jendi's father, an old hajji. They took him to Dawlat-abad and put him in jail. They said they would release him only if Karim Jendi turned himself in. That was in late winter, seven months before Ramadan.

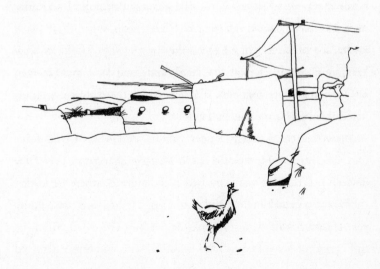

Karim Jendi, meantime, was on the lam, mostly in Oqa. Oqa seemed a good place to hide from the law.

"No one ever finds anyone in Oqa," bragged Manon the shopkeeper. He himself had come to the village to hide, seventeen years earlier, from the draft board that had tracked him down in Khairabad where he had been a sharecropper, and ordered him to report for duty in Mazar-e-Sharif. He had rolled his belongings into a carpet, corralled his few goats and sheep, and trekked to Oqa across the lonely wastes worn into bald grooves by shepherds' slippers. Here he built a cob house that faced south, faced any potential search party, faced the cemetery full of children's graves, faced the mountains full of graves of invaders, faced the rest of Afghanistan.

From the tiny mercantile he ran out of a narrow side room of his house, Manon sold Korean cigarettes, wooden Russian matches in boxes decorated with drawings of biplanes, Pakistani acetamino-phen in tablets, Crown safety razor blades, soap, sugar, dirty black raisins for pilau and dried chickpeas by the kilo, padlocks with keys, some veterinary medicine, hard candy, and condoms. The men of Oqa did not use condoms. These were for the children, who in-flated them into long pale balloons.

Now that there was no longer a draft, Manon was free to leave Oqa. He did not. He stocked up in Mazar-e-Sharif once every few days and carried his wares by taxi to Khairabad, where he loaded them onto a camel and walked it to Oqa. He had two sons, three-year-old Azizullah, who still took suck at least twice daily from the full breasts of Manon's quiet and beautiful wife, and fifteen-year-old

Rakhmatullah, whom the shopkeeper was teaching to read with the help of a geographical brochure about Afghanistan that had lost its binding years ago and was now a pile of single pages stacked on the shop floor in no particular order. "The book has nothing about Oqa," Manon explained. "It is mostly about mines and factories." He was the only man in the village who knew how to read.

There were other papers in the room. On the floor next to the geographical brochure that did not mention Oqa lay Manon's voter's card, punctured four times, one for each time he had gone to the polls. He toed it, smiled at the joke that it seemed to him. "Nothing," he summed up.

And on the wall, next to the shelf with two glass syringes—Manon had trained as a nurse before he had become a draft dodger and used one of the hypodermics to administer shots to sick livestock, the other to humans, for free—hung Rakhmatullah's two beautiful drawings in colored pencil on writing paper. In each drawing a pomegranate tree grew in a pot. Each tree was heavy with enormous red fruit.

Pomegranates. They would never grow in Oqa. The boy could have drawn waterfalls. He could have drawn unicorns.

The men of Oqa drank their tea and shook their heads from side to side at the injustice of life that in their experience always favored the rich and always punished the poor.

"All the people who are working for the government know this is not right. But they are just taking Khan Geldi's orders."

"Khan Geldi paid the police to arrest Karim Jendi."

"Five hundred dollars!"

"They eat money!"

"The dreaded Karim Jendi is just a poor goatherd with four goats."

"He's a good man. A Turkoman. We are from the same tribe. We are from the same land. We are relatives."

Qaqa Satar, no kin of Turkomans, clicked his tongue and said that Karim Jendi was a dangerous bandit who would kidnap me and sell me to the Taliban. He said Karim Jendi was the reason he had refused to let me spend the night in Oqa in the spring.

Amin Bai spat out the cigarette butt that had burnt to a rank stub in the corner of his mouth and spat a tiny white speck of saliva after it.

"Karim is my friend," he said to me. "Don't worry about Karim. If I don't give an order, he can't do anything to you."

The last sentence made me nervous. I asked Amin Bai why he would ever give anyone an order to do anything to me. He laughed and said nothing.

The plane looped round and round overhead, and we watched and watched until at last the plane was gone.

It had not bombed Oqa.

I did meet Karim Jendi once. He was squatting in the corner of Baba Nazar's *namad*. He seemed in his forties, fatigued. He wore a tattered brown *shalwar kameez*, a gray vest, a tartan turban. His sandals of molded plastic sat in the dust at the edge of the blanket, heels together, toes facing away from the rug, ready to be slipped on in a hurry: a fugitive's footwear. His shirt's elbows had patches. His feet had sores. He looked weak. He owned twenty goats. His first name, Karim, meant "giving, generous." His second name, Jendi, in Farsi meant "whore." Uttered together, they sounded funny. Everybody laughed whenever someone would mention Karim Jendi's full name.

The unfortunate man with the unfortunate name sat on Baba Nazar's *namad* and reached inside the chest pocket of his vest and pulled out a transparent pink plastic bag and produced out of it a sheaf of creased and finger-soiled papers and unfolded it and handed me the papers one by one.

A letter from a lawyer to the provincial prosecutor's office in Mazar-e-Sharif requesting the release of the goatherd's father.

Three letters from the provincial governor to the police chief in Dawlatabad demanding the immediate release of the goatherd's father, dated spring and summer.

A deed to the farmland Karim Jendi said was his property and Khan Geldi was said to claim as his.

The goatherd could not read, but he knew what the papers said. He also knew what they were worth. Nothing.

Swallows streaked through the blue. Karim Jendi, the fugitive murderer, the dangerous insurgent, the savage bandit, the slandered pauper, the generous whore, wept on Baba Nazar's felt rug.

"My father is almost seventy years old. A long time ago he was a wheat and rice farmer, and had a hundred and fifty goats, but now he doesn't do much. I'm afraid he will die in jail."

He looked at the barchans full of inaccessible gold, at the opal sky full of freedom and birds, at the landscape that had stayed the same since the mythical times when wealthy landlords who had tyrannized poor villagers were always punished and reprieve for the destitute always hinged on magic.

"Ever since I went into hiding, I have not earned anything. I would have sold all my animals, but because of the drought, the price of animals is low. I'd only get about a thousand dollars. I owe relatives and friends two thousand dollars already. I keep asking my friends for money. If I'm in jail, who will look after my animals?"

That Ramadan, the police did arrest Karim Jendi at last. They cornered him in Khairabad one day when he came to check on his house. He put up no resistance, made no effort to run. He must have been too tired. Or maybe his plastic sandals gave out. The police took him to jail in Dawlatabad. They did not release his father.

"Do you feel better about spending a night in Oqa now that Karim Jendi is in jail?" I asked Qaqa Satar. We were on our way to Oqa and, as usual, Baba Nazar had invited me to stay. I should have been able to predict the answer. The driver had grown more skittish about leaving Mazar-e-Sharif as the year had waxed. On many days when I wanted to hit the road, he would need to visit with a relative from out of town, or attend an important meeting at his mosque in the city, or suggest we hire a police escort. Maybe he was protecting me from some dangers I had no way of knowing about. Maybe he was protecting himself from the anger of his own Pashtun clansmen, many of whom either supported or belonged to the strengthening insurgency and probably frowned upon his employment by a foreigner, a Westerner, a woman. Maybe both. His Luger had migrated from its spot behind the hand brake to a nook in his lap. A couple of times, on country roads that wound past patches of drought-shriveled cotton fields, he had cocked it at motorcycle riders who quivered, miragelike, on the blanched and speckled plains.

Qaqa Satar was observing the fast with piety. On the first day of Ramadan, he had stopped smoking opium and even hashish. Opioid withdrawal gave him terrible muscle cramps, nausea, and chills. Not being able to toke accelerated his anxieties. Going cold turkey on an empty stomach and with a tongue sandpapered by thirst made him glum and ill-tempered. He snapped: "Is there no more war now that Osama bin Laden is dead?"

Then he drove me to Dawlatabad, and there, at the piss-fouled concrete gate of the district police headquarters behind which Karim Jendi and his father were interned, he pulled over, killed the engine, and quit.

~~~~

A nd who could blame him? Now even Oqa was feeling the tremors of war. Village boys and men left for the desert to collect thistle and returned heaped with troublesome rumors of skulking gunmen, of roadside bombings, of some other new and inarticulable threats. Relatives came to visit from other villages, trailing a kind of limbic angst. The men of Oqa roosted on Baba Nazar's bed four in a row and made the old springs sink almost to where the hunter's skinny kid goat trussed to one of the bed legs was lying in the shade of the rusty frame, and more men squatted in the goat droppings next to the bed, and all of them took turns listing to one another the latest worrisome news they had heard. The men clicked their tongues. Like timepieces in some baleful clockmaker's store ticking out the approach of trouble.

"Thk, thk, thk." Thawra's sickle echoed from inside the loom room, where the woman was knotting carmine and burgundy wool into lotuses and flying eagles, lacing the yarn around the warp of worries and hopes, weaving around the shortage of tan thread.

"Security is getting bad. There are lots of Taliban."

"Not inside the village, but outside, yes, plenty of them."

"Here in our village, the people are united. If any strangers come, they won't let them enter."

"But they are coming to the villages near us."

"They killed a teacher in Siogert."

"They shot at the village militia checkpoint in Shahrak. Taliban came at night, the men fired at one another, but no one was hurt. No one knows where they came from."

"This place is safe, and Karaghuzhlah. Other places are not safe."

"People say that travelers on the road are attacked by the Taliban. I have never seen them. But I hear that the road is not safe."

That the war was escalating and that thousands of people were dying in it all over the country were indisputable facts. But in Afghanistan each fact was multifaceted and truth was never simple. What the Oqans considered safe or dangerous hinged upon their individual histories and the village history as a whole, upon their tribal relations and social status, their ethnic prejudices, upon the mythicized narrative of real and perceived transgressions and kindnesses committed by them and by others that went back years and decades and centuries. Karaghuzhlah was safe for Amin Bai but not Khairabad because during the Soviet occupation, Amin Bai had been in charge of a troop of mujaheddin and had ordered that troop to assassinate a wealthy and influential Khairabad landlord, and the landlord's family wanted requital. Karaghuzhlah was safe for Amin Bai, but it was no longer safe for Qaqa Satar's cousin Naushir, who had been born and raised in that village, because he worked as a detective in the Afghan border police and was therefore a collaborator with the government the insurgency had vouched to topple, a traitor to the guerrillas' sense of national pride. Qaqa Satar, who still was working with me at the time of this conversation, would in a day or two define the boundaries of his own safety and decide that his car was off-limits to me. And when whichever of the sides fighting this particular phase of the Khorasan's everlasting war would come out the winner, the war would not end but merely shift course to accommodate all the intricacies of the newly accumulated panoply of offenses and invite the slighted to get their redress and trespass against someone else. And so on.

The only danger the Oqans could not rationalize or predict came from the foreign invaders who flew their planes and helicopters over the desert for no reason the Oqans could justify, and from men who strapped bombs to their bicycles or belts or hid them in their turbans or in their vests and took lives wholesale and at random, without regard for family ties or political allegiances or ethnic affiliations. Suicide bombers were this particular war's great equalizers.

I was sitting before the men on Baba Nazar's butchering block, taking notes, listening. My history in the desert was different from the Oqans'. It was nonexistent: I had no tribal enemies, no old-time allies. Yet it was also the millennial communal history of foreigners who had come here and who often had perished here, even when their pilgrimages were well intentioned, as was rarely the case. Qul Nazar, a slat-ribbed elder who grew a dozen sparse white chin hairs on the vertex of his triangular face, nodded at me.

"When you come here, don't the Taliban say anything to you?"

I said they did not. I said that if the Taliban had met me on the road long enough to say anything to me, they probably would not let me go to Oqa. If the Taliban had met me on the road, they probably would not let me go anywhere but where they wanted me to go, because the Taliban were kidnapping foreigners those days for ransom. Not only that, bandits who had nothing to do with the insurgency also were kidnapping foreigners and selling them to the Taliban.

In silence, Qul Nazar and I considered my vulnerability. Measured my chances against the chances of the village boys who tramped through treacherous vastnesses daily. Of baby Zakrullah whose parents were too intoxicated to notice his latest deterioration. Of all the Oqans, including those not yet born upon this horseshoe-shaped rise in the plains, who will dream of long and exquisite journeys and beautiful life elsewhere and who probably will spend their whole lives toiling on the cruel hummock the way their fathers and their fathers' fathers had toiled. I had a ticket for an airplane, a magic carpet ride that would carry me out of Afghanistan, beyond the rectangular borders of Oqa's world. They did not.

The elder chewed his gums for a spell, then said: "It would be good if you at least had a gun."

Amin Bai rose from the bed and the bedsprings readjusted with a groan. All the men watched him. The kid goat raised its head at the noise and lowered it again.

"When there's fighting," the Commander said, "there is no law. The law is your Kalashnikov. Wherever you shoot, there you rule."

He took a soft pack of cigarettes out of his vest pocket and shook a cigarette upward and stuck it between his teeth and nodded at Amanullah for a matchbox. I held out a lighter, but he refused it with a stopping motion of his hand. He took out a wooden match from the matchbox Amanullah handed to him and struck it and cupped the small flame up to his cigarette and inhaled and blew white smoke through his nose in two long white echelons and said to me: "At the time of the Communists, it was better. You knew who was your friend and who was your enemy. Now you can't tell enemy from friend."

His eyes tapered into two tiny black grains.

"At the time of the Russians, we didn't have suicide bombings. It's you foreigners who came and brought with you all this terrorism."

And he stomped off.

᠈᠈᠈᠈

Was Amin Bai enemy or friend? His extensive yet vaguely defined power perturbed me. Whom did the Commander command? There were no men under arms in Oqa. How did he make a living? What paid for the gas for his Iranian motorbike, the rice for his family's dinners, his cigarettes, his children's plastic shoes, his opium? All other families in Oqa earned the bulk of their income by selling the carpets the women wove. I never met Amin Bai's wife, but I knew that she did not weave—not in her house, not in anyone else's. Nor did his sole surviving daughter, Mahsad Gul, who often flitted through the village with her friend Hazar Gul, the daughter of Choreh Gul and Choreh, and with a covey of other girls their age—or else dallied barefoot, carrying on her hip the Commander's toddler, Amrullah, who always wore layers of home-stitched green and purple quilted shirts and vests on his back and almost never wore any clothes below his waist no matter the weather and who often urinated down the side and front of Mahsad Gul's dress, but she paid that no attention. Amin Bai's teenage son, Ismatullah, harvested calligonum to barter for rice and oil, but not very often. Mostly he spent days ambling about the village, aiming his slingshot at pale desert larks that danced up from the dunes like airborne sand clumps, or else playing with his cell phone. His cell phone. Few Oqa households had cell phones; Baba Nazar and Amanullah shared one. But Ismatullah, at fourteen, had his own, and so did Amin Bai. What paid for those? In the past the Commander had owned some goats and sheep, but two years earlier he had sold his livestock, and now only a couple of pack camels remained.

"Our expenses were not paid by the animals," he explained.

"By what, then?" I asked.

Amin Bai's smile curved around his cigarette.

"I buy and sell things."

"Which things?"

He did not answer. He rarely answered personal questions. But many times I saw men lie on their sides in the guestroom of his house, smoking opium on soiled mattresses. I figured he was the village dealer.

And one more thing. A police detective in Dawlatabad—the very department that had arrested first Karim Jendi's elderly father then the fugitive goatherd himself—told me that Amin Bai called him every day. "To report on the security situation in the village," the officer said.

The Commander, the village snitch.

This man who cradled his Korean cigarettes in a crooked thin smile may have been the one tenuous link between his hamlet and the rest of Afghanistan—the Afghanistan beyond the visible desert, beyond the familiar villages full of Turkoman relatives, beyond Dawlatabad's Carpet Row where merchants sold the Oqans their wool and bought their carpets, the Afghanistan of ever-changing and forever-indifferent officialdom that seemed to know little about Oqa and care even less. He chose what to report and whom to inform on, whose visits to the village to keep secret (Karim Jendi's) and whose to disclose (at least some of mine, according to the officer in Dawlatabad). In the Khorasan, where law and villainy were concepts obscure and frequently interchangeable, knowing when and which information to withhold could mean survival; it could also mean death. Was he responsible for Oqa's isolation because it suited him, preserved his importance, kept the peace, at least for now? Or was he its victim, the same as all the other Oqa fathers who had buried their young children in unmarked graves in the village cemetery? Maybe, I thought, he was both.

T wo nights after Qaqa Satar quit, an earthquake shook, shook, shook the carpeted concrete floor under my tick mattress in Mazar-e-Sharif like some subterranean giant trying to rock me to sleep. Shook the glass in the window and the pewter dishes left unwashed in the kitchen after a Ramadan breakfast of reheated left-over rice and okra, shook the moon, shook the desert. Northern Afghanistan was a land of extreme seismicity, laced with tectonic faults and balanced on two plates—the Arabian and the Indian—that were shifting northward constantly and at different speeds and forever subducting under Eurasia: an allegory furnished by the universe itself.

But in the morning, the sun rose over the Khorasan as though nothing at all had happened, white-hot. In that chalky glare in an unpaved Mazar-e-Sharif street three riders climbed into a white and yellow Toyota Corolla and started on a two-hour journey north to Oqa.

Over the steering wheel wrapped in a faux sheepskin cover that occasionally shed dirty white wisps of polyester into his lap hunched Qasim, the twenty-two-year-old driver who smiled most of the time and bathed rarely and always wore the same ecru *shalwar kameez* and soiled gray waistcoat.

Straight-backed in the backseat because women in Afghanistan did not ride in front sat the young and unflappable Hakima, who was translating for me that day. Hakima had grown up in exile in Iran, held a brand-new bachelor's degree in business administration from the American University in Kyrgyzstan, and was a city girl;

she had sass and she had style. Whenever she and I strolled through Mazar-e-Sharif together, the men who squatted in the shade of their shops would follow her with greedy eyes and whisper to one another that she surely must be a foreigner. For her first trip to one of the world's most impoverished villages in one of the world's oldest war zones, Hakima wore a lilac headscarf, a hip-length belted purple trench coat, skinny blue jeans, a leather purse, and strappy white heels.

I huddled next to her, sweating already in dark and spreading blotches through my gray cotton *shalwar kameez* and plain beige veil and cheap rubber sandals, an outfit that I told myself made me inconspicuous but that in reality was a mismatch only the most destitute Afghan woman would have stooped to, someone who picked her clothes out of garbage heaps that rotted on street corners—for beneath their burqas, Afghan women took great care to coordinate the colors of their headscarves and their dress, particularly in Mazar, the Milan of Afghanistan. My hosts were of the unanimous opinion that most of my clothes were ugly and told me so, even the men. The women sometimes added that my breasts were no good.

Squeezed into the taxi that flew one sooty and shredded red ribbon from the radio antenna and another from the grille to protect the passengers against evil spirits, the three of us looked an outlandish and misplaced carnival, an ill-assorted troupe of circus freaks, a band of castoffs from three separate eras that the Earth's nocturnal rumblings had loosened all at once upon this corner of Central Asia. That was all right. These plains had witnessed stranger spectacles before. King Alexander's Hellenic cavalry in purple tunics and plumed helmets. The Golden Horde, flying yak-tail banners and swilling fermented horse milk and reeking of fire smoke and wearing armor of cured yak hide. The Hindu pundits deployed by British India to map mountain passes, dressed as Muslim holy men, their compasses and sextants concealed in beads and walking staffs. A succession of Europeans pretending not to be: Lieutenant Arthur Connolly, the British spy who had coined the phrase the "Great Game," traveled across Afghanistan in 1830 disguised as an Indian merchant; Lieutenant Henry Pottinger, who had snooped around Transoxiana for the crown twenty years before Connolly, passed himself off as a Tatar horse dealer; Sir Alexander Burnes, who believed that "no European traveler has ever journeyed in such countries without suspicion," during his trip from Punjab to Kabul in 1832 wore Afghan clothes and made his four Indian companions do the same. And to what avail the masquerade? A mob in Kabul eventually hacked Burnes to death. The emir of Bukhara beheaded Connolly in a public square. I took comfort in knowing that Pottinger died in retirement in Malta. Lately, jumpy and haunted NATO soldiers scuttled across the long-suffering landscape like some postapocalyptic alien warriors, with every bit of their skin and even much of their pixelated camouflage uniforms invisible behind body armor, reflective sunglasses, gloves, helmets, chin guards, neck guards, knee guards, ballistic groin protectors, boots, and more often than not their entire bodies entombed in outsize armored apparatuses stubbled with gun barrels and antennae and tinted electronic gadgets whose unchaste purpose, many Afghans believed, was to X-ray through women's clothes.

Onward, then. Qasim bent over his furry wheel. Road gravel sang Bollywood tunes under the tires of his taxi. Behind us, to the south, mountaintops flounced with a thin glacial smear faded into the haze. The car rattled past the sandbagged northern boundary of Mazar-e-Sharif where a police officer in a gray fleece uniform dozed behind a concrete blast wall, past the lowlands where the city dumped her refuse into black-rimmed lakes of stunning turquoise putrefaction, past the dirt track that dead-ended at the adobe beehive of the Asfakhan Shrine beneath which in a low ziggurat painted pea green lay buried a Muslim holy man named Mir Sangin. The tomb of this saint, who had died more than eight centuries earlier, was said to cure mental ailments. Worshippers pilgrimed to the shrine each Wednesday. They knelt and prostrated before the tomb and chained themselves to the metal railing that surrounded it and wept and moaned and prayed and sometimes urinated upon themselves while their desperate relatives suffered the stench in set-jaw silence and hoped for a miracle. When we passed the turnoff to the shrine, Qasim let go of the wheel and closed his eyes and drew both hands over his clean-shaven face in blessing. Soon after that, our road became barely discernible in the flat and empty desert that gazed blankly at a sky just as blank. A falcon freewheeled in hot air.

Qasim was living with his wife and toddler daughter across the street from my rental room in Mazar, but he had grown up in Karaghuzhlah where his parents and siblings still lived, and he drove there often. He said he knew the desert well. About an hour north of Mazar-e-Sharif, he turned in his seat and beamed at me.

"Anna!"

"Yes?"

"Where is the road to Oqa?"

Where, indeed? There was no road. Only, in a certain light, at a certain angle, lustrous furrows upon the parched alkali where herders' sandals had worn the dust to a gloss, and sometimes, depending on the strength of the wind and on the recent traffic patterns through the desert, some motorcycle tracks. Forty minutes of that, jolting west-northwest, and then to the north there would appear the dunes and the cemetery of children and elders and the hillock of Oqa. Then another twenty minutes of crossing corduroy fallows from there to the village. To reach the village by car from Mazar-e-Sharif you bounced on the gravel road north for an hour or so and then turned west. Where?

"How about . . . here!"

Qasim swerved left.

"Here?"

I squinted at the land, the funereal whiteness of it. There were absolutely no landmarks. The morning glare was eating away at the horizon the way a slow fire eats at the corners of a burning page, almost imperceptible, consuming the edges in a barely visible radiant hairline border. It flattened everything, leveled whichever hillocks or distant cob ruins were sometimes, not on this day, amplified by diffraction. The hard-packed dust before the taxi shone like polished chalk. I was lost.

Stories about getting lost in deserts, in cars. Of draining and drinking radiator fluid. Gasoline. Urine. Of setting cars on fire so that someone—here, in these plains, who? NATO helicopter gunships? Taliban raiders?—would notice and come to the rescue. Of parents killing their young son to spare him the final agonies. He had become so dehydrated his tongue had swelled, and he could no longer swallow even if there had been anything to drink. In the August heat of the Khorasan, with no shelter, in the sun, we would dehydrate through sweat and through breathing beyond recovery within four or five hours—or less, because we had not had anything to drink since before dawn, since Qasim and Hakima were fasting and so was I, for the sake of collegial austerity, for the attraction of living within limits, the nonbinding seduction of the rituals of others. We had an almost full tank of gas and some bottled water in the trunk.

"Sure," I said.

Then I asked Qasim to drive in a line as straight as possible and shut my eyes against the glare, and for the next forty minutes I tried to will Oqa into existence.

And there it was.

The cemetery with the sole plywood marker buckled to our south. The pronounced footpath tacked from it, northwest and then east, to the white wasp's nest of clay homes. The undulating gold-specked dunes behind it, the ever-encroaching sea. But there was something unfamiliar about the approach. There was new sand everywhere—new miniature barchans and new flawless sheets of sand like iced-over ponds and corrugated patches like furrowed sand fields, new sand dimples and new rippled sand hummocks where before there had been none, blown in by the wind over the previous two days, or else joggled loose by the earthquake the night before. Sand blocked the climb up the hillock of Oqa. Qasim revved the engine once, twice. And then the yellow and white taxi, with its red good-luck ribbons and its hairy steering wheel, was stuck.

We flung open the car doors and stepped out into the sand that billowed about our feet and clicked our tongues. The car was tilted into the side of the knoll like a prairie dog frozen halfway into its burrowing act. Stuck in shit, for this was the north slope of the hummock, the slope the Oqans used as an outhouse. Stuck also in gold. Bored two feet nose-first into the untapped riches that teased Amanullah's imagination and stoked his hopes of flight. Already a small crowd of children had tumbled down the hillside and assembled around us, tinkling with their shiny amulets and waving and laughing and pointing and beckoning: *"Khola jan, khola jan, salaam!"* Auntie, they called me, and my heart quavered. And to their urgings and giggles, we the three hapless and incongruously wardrobed jesters hiked the short rise to Baba Nazar's house. Boston rushed out of the loom room where she had been sorting through old skeins and balls of carpet wool left over from some past carpets to see if she could salvage enough tan thread for Thawra to finish her *yusufi.* She clenched me in her skeletal embrace. Most of the villagers were gone, she said. Amanullah had taken the family camels to a far pasture because all the grazing nearby had been devoured by animals or burnt by the drought. Baba Nazar had gone to the dunes to see if the desert would yield a rabbit or two for dinner. Thawra had gone with the children to visit her family in Khairabad.

"Everyone, everyone," the old woman said; everyone had gone to look for food, for kindling, for animal feed, or to crash the iftar dinners of wealthier relatives in other villages—because not observing the fast did not exclude the Oqans from partaking in the ritual reward for the long hours of abstinence since abstinence was how they lived every month, holy or not.

Everyone was gone, Boston said, and no one to help us out of the sand except the Commander, the only able-bodied man who had stayed in the village that day and had not gone to forage for food because the Commander never foraged for anything.

"There he comes!" Boston pointed, and grinned.

Amin Bai was shuffling across the village to greet us. Contrails of fine dust danced behind his rubber slippers. In his arms he was carrying a wooden door.

⟩⟩⟩⟩

Many Ramadans ago in Shor Teppeh, on the northern edge of the barchan belt that separated Oqa from the Oxus, there lived carpenters who carved out of juniper and tamarisk amazing things. Filigreed chests with complex mortise-and-tenon locks. Chairs with long backs whittled into interlacing openwork octagons that rested upon stout legs just tall enough to elevate the chairs' occupants above the floor so that they could sit comfortably cross-legged as if they were sitting on cushions or tick mattresses. Doors chip-carved into precious multitudes of leaves and flowers.

The Shor Teppeh craftsmen preserved an artisanal tradition that in Transoxiana dated back to Tamerlane—Emir Timur, the Father of the Turks, the crippled sociopath who was crowned emperor in Balkh in 1370, who designated his carpet as his royal surrogate, and who combined a savage, maniacal bloodlust with singular love for and patronage of the arts. For thirty-five years he expanded his domain from the Mediterranean and Black seas to the Persian Gulf to India, fighting wars at whim with a bandy-legged army of mercenaries who were paid exclusively in spoils and who slaughtered prisoners by the hundred thousand and mixed their skulls with clay and erected from that abominable amalgam enormous pyramids; who stampeded enemy lines with camels set aflame; and who, at least on one occasion, at Smyrna, catapulted the severed heads of the defeated Knights Hospitaller into the fleet that had sailed up to the city to rescue the crusaders. Tamerlane did not decimate the human race the way Genghis Khan had, but he did kill seventeen million people in a world of four hundred million. During the same thirty-five years, having moved the Mongol capital to Samarkand, Tamerlane meticulously imported from the different lands he had conquered assorted craftsmen who built Samarkand's grand mosques bedecked with polychrome tiles and initiated one of the most glorious periods in Islamic art. Because beauty is blind to bloodshed and is, in fact, often sustained by it, or else the world as we know it would not be.

Six hundred years later, the Khorasan still embraced indescribable beauty and ruthless violence and ruinous penury at once. Bulbous-domed mosques blinked impassively in the sun at street bombings that hurled a mess of charred and shredded human flesh at their lapis tiles. Tinsmiths rumbaed sheets of aluminum into ornamented trunks and strongboxes to the syncopation of firefights. And on the edge of a war zone, the pauperized Oqans wove the world's handsomest carpets and counted among their few possessions the gorgeous Shor Teppeh xyloglyphy.

The mortise-and-tenon chests were the most common. Every other house in the village seemed to have one. Amanullah had one in his room: an imposing hexahedron of dark wood that had been Boston's trousseau when she had married Baba Nazar. Interweaving scallops connected into hexagons that in their turn were linked by low-relief balusters fretted with yet more tiny runeations. Inside the chest, which they kept padlocked, Baba Nazar and Boston kept their money, the hunter's disintegrated and frasslike birth certificate that had been issued by a government long gone and that was no longer valid, and an American zinc-alloy military challenge coin that read "Robert M. Gates, Secretary of Defense" on one side and "The United States of America, Department of Defense" on the other. Baba Nazar believed the challenge coin was a medal. He said American troops had awarded it to his brother Ala Nazar, a police officer who had served in Jalalabad, for risking his life when he had helped capture a low-level Taliban commander. I did not have the heart to tell him that American troops used such coins mostly to elicit free drinks from their buddies. A handheld mirror for a gold nugget. A worthless trinket for a lifetime of worry. The hunter showed it occasionally to his guests, and they passed it from hand to hand with great care and nodded and said it was a beautiful and precious thing indeed.

It was possible that the woodworkers still lived in Shor Teppeh. But no one I met in Oqa had ever seen one, and everyone assured me that the chests in their possession were a hundred or two hundred or three hundred years old. These were probably uninformed estimates, but they were easy to believe. The blackened wood on the chests looked antiquated. The trees that once had been abundant in the oases along the river had been cut down for cooking fires or swallowed up by the ever-encroaching sand. Boston had no opinion regarding the age of her trousseau other than that her mother had owned it forever before giving it to her; Baba Nazar said it was more than a century old. It was the only piece of furniture the couple owned save for the looted bed.

The door Amin Bai was carrying had come from Shor Teppeh as well. It was the descendant of the cypress panel the carpenters' Timurid ancestors had hewn in fifteenth-century Samarkand that was on display, more than half a millennium later, in Gallery 455 of the Metropolitan Museum of Art in New York. The same delicate and fluid tendrils that wove into symmetrical bas-relief gardens. The same calligraphic clusters of flowers and fruit. It was a treasure, an objet d'art. It had been painted pale blue to thwart jinxes. Securing it with his left armpit and elbow, the Commander shook hands with me, with Qasim, with Hakima, murmured the polite chant of a greeting, and then slid down the side of the hummock on his heels, parting the fine sand in two parallel ruts the way the ducks Baba Nazar would very rarely hunt on the Amu Darya peeled the surface of the water with their webbed feet at touchdown, and with all the momentum gathered from such a descent he wedged the door under the taxi's right front wheel. Six hundred years of art history, echoes of pyramids of skulls, legends of unbelievable and unbelievably gory conquests, jammed under the radial tire of a 1997 Toyota Corolla. Except the door was too thick. It wouldn't quite fit.

Amin Bai turned to Qasim.

"Got a jack, son?" he asked.

The door didn't help. Nor did the tarp on which Boston shucked almonds, nor the armloads of calligonum the children had brought at Amin Bai's orders, nor Amin Bai's and my shoveling. ("You work like a man! Good!") Some boys came over to help push the car, but it just rocked. I suggested deflating the tires, but Qasim said no because he didn't have a pump. He had stopped smiling and kept stepping on the gas, and the tires spun and dislodged from the scalding sand browned shreds of the old cloth village women used to catch their menstrual blood and shards of blue-glazed pots. The shards looked ancient, but they could have come from crockery of any age—a year old, a thousand years old, a hundred. Like malnourished babies born old-looking. The car now rested on its undercarriage.

At last Amin Bai stabbed the shovel into a small dune next to the car and came over to me, hand extended for the shaking. He reached for his Korean cigarettes, shook one out of the soft pack, offered it to me. I took it, fished a lighter out of my purse, offered the Commander a light in cupped hands. He took it. Friend, then, at least for now, I thought.

A hot gale blew from the northwest across a desert lepered with thistle tufts. We sat on our haunches next to the taxi and watched the dunes in the satisfied silence of laborers who had done all they could for a cause. The dunes had won. Then we shimmied up the hummock and went to sit in Baba Nazar's house because inside it was somewhat cool, while Qasim walked to the westernmost end of the village where the cell phone signal was stronger, dialed his father in Karaghuzhlah, and asked him to send over a tractor.

The earthen floor in Boston's bedroom was covered with a straw mat and there we sat. We rested our backs on hard corduroy pillows and squinted at one another across the beams of dusty light that thrust through the windows and crisscrossed the room like trip wire. Above us, from the rafters, the couple's domestic things hung. An unfinished slingshot. A plate of something wrapped in a green and fuchsia homespun headscarf. A sieve holding three loaves of fresh nan. A stick driven into the wall pierced a piece of paper with five sewing needles stuck in it. The surviving bow of Baba Nazar's prescription glasses hooked over a nail. On a shelf built into an alcove, next to the case holding the hunter's Soviet binoculars, a golden handful of onions. Some girls had squeezed past one another into the room and stood by the door, giggling in shy whispers. They were watching Hakima. A city lady. Her clothes so fine, her eyebrows tweezed to such perfect narrow arches, her skin so white. At last, Mahsad Gul, the Commander's daughter, moved forward and, full of sudden courage, stepped into my sweaty sandals, then into Hakima's heels. The other girls watched us. Had we noticed? Was it all right? When we said nothing, the rest of the girls tried on Hakima's nice shoes, too.

Ismatullah, the Commander's firstborn, wandered in, pushed past his sister, bowed to the adults. Once, in the winter, the boy had given me a blue glass bead shaped like a teardrop, or a human heart. His friend Hairullah gave me a bead as well, a flat dark-red circle with the name of the Prophet inscribed on both sides. Gifts, the boys had explained, trinkets they had found in the desert. I had strung them on a thread and wore that around my neck until the thread ripped, many months later. Now Ismatullah wanted something in return.

"Auntie."

"Yes?"

"Can you bring me from the city a SIM card for my cell phone with Turkoman songs on it?" he asked, in Farsi.

"A what? A SIM card?"

"*Doo jee bee.*"

I thought he had switched to Turkoman, which I did not understand.

"*Which* kind?"

Amin Bai cut in. My obtuseness irritated him.

"Mem-ree card," he said, in English. "Two GB."

Father and son. Unlettered, thin, fatigued-looking in their dirty *shalwar kameez* and soiled white skullcaps, their feet dark and seamy from always being bare in molded rubber sandals, explaining electronics to me, in English. Their lives forever pincered between ageless privation and advanced modernity. Not until then had I heard of two-gigabyte memory cards for cell phones that could store songs.

Boston meantime had unfolded a corner of her houndstooth tablecloth and placed upon it a loaf of bread and a saucer of fresh yogurt: one of her camels was in milk. Chipped glass teacups came out, and the pale green thermos painted with tulips. Hakima, hand on heart, refused the elevenses. Ramadan, she said.

Boston wouldn't hear of it.

"Eat." And she pushed the saucer closer to the translator. "God knows you have to eat something. No one can fast in this." Amin Bai and I were already ripping bits of nan crust and dipping them into the yogurt. It tasted like liquid moonlight.

And then Qasim returned and reported that the tractor carrying four laborers and many meters of heavy-duty rope would be in Oqa to fetch us in an hour—and also that his father, Hassan Khan, the Hazara commander from Karaghuzhlah, was sending his salaams to Amin Bai, the Turkoman commander from Oqa, his dear old friend.

The Commander, who had been lying propped up on his left elbow and eating with his right hand, sat up with an ornate litany of a Farsi greeting, this time heartfelt. And suddenly, unexpectedly, I had a history in the desert beyond the ignoble history of foreigners, a reason to be present in Oqa beyond squibbling notes and sketching: I had, through the young taxi driver I had hired, acquired an ally, a confederate, a Hazara warlord who had been Amin Bai's war buddy.

That afternoon, before the tractor pulled Qasim's taxi out of the dune, Amin Bai asked me to bring him binoculars from America, "to see far in the desert." To hunt with Baba Nazar, or maybe to watch for intruders, he did not say.

❧

Two days later, Qasim took me to Karaghuzhlah to meet his father. We drove past Naushir's house, past the pale green mosque to which Taliban riders had delivered their letters instruct-

ing the villagers to pay the ten percent religious tax to the militia, past a water pump where two small girls were loading yellow jerry cans that once had held cooking oil and now held well water onto a wooden cart pulled by a balding donkey. In the Hazara quarter of Karaghuzhlah, in the northwest corner of the village, Qasim steered the taxi across a short land bridge barely wide enough for his car. The bridge spanned an irrigation ditch dry and cracked like broken stoneware, and it ended at a sheetmetal gate. A teenage farmhand opened the gate for us, and we parked in a small courtyard next to an outhouse. A cloud of flies rose in furious and restless scarves from a stinking mottle of sheep offal left to rot on some withered grass.

A low wall separated this from the inner yard planted with rows of mulberry trees and poplars and twisted grapevines that sagged under unripe fruit. A two-story house with large wooden sashes painted blue. A lacy flutter of white curtains. A porch of white-washed mud. In the back, a tandoor sunken into a clay platform for Qasim's worried mother, Khanum, to squat upon when she baked bread. Hassan Khan himself, his beard indigo black and his skin darkened from fieldwork, smiling his son's smile from the doorway: "Welcome, welcome." A couple of fat-tailed sheep. A crop-eared sheepdog asleep in the shade of a water tank. Some thin and bossy chickens on long legs. A duck. And, beneath a trellis, *en pointe* on fowl down and animal refuse, two tragic silver question marks, two ideograms of heaven, as if their presence somehow could sanctify things: two demoiselle cranes.

I stopped to stare. The cranes were preening. Their wings had been clipped.

"These were a present from Oqa," the warlord said. "My friend Amin Bai gave them to me."

The poisoned cranes.

I said: "I know. I know these birds. I have seen them in Oqa."

"You like them?"

"They are very beautiful."

I felt violated.

"Here." The man started toward the cranes. "Take one. Take it to America."

But I thanked him for his kindness, and thanked him also for sending the tractor to rescue us the other day, and told him I would not be allowed to bring a crane on the airplane with me.

~~~

The melon season arrived in the Khorasan that month as always, heedless of Ramadan or violence or hardship, the fruit's cool pulpy fragrance a timepiece that denoted August. In the ocher fields that canted from the Hindu Kush, the melons, where the heat had cleft their pale green and golden skins, looked like severed heads discarded by war.

In the early ninth century, "the crisp, deliciously refreshing melons of Balkh Province . . . were placed in leaden molds packed with ice and thus sent to grace the table of the Caliph in Baghdad," the historian Nancy Dupree wrote in her 1967 guidebook to Northern Afghanistan. In the thirteenth century, Genghis Khan's Khitan advisor Yelu Ch'u-Ts'ai marveled at melons "as big as a horse's head."

Eight hundred years later, the melons were just as big, gourdfuls of condensed sunshine. In the evenings, when Mazar-e-Sharif cooled off and orange smog hung in the streets almost solid like unfiltered honey, melon vendors arranged their fruit in roadside pyramids and illuminated them with kerosene lanterns and single-bulb lamps fed by small generators, and shoppers looking for a sweet finish to their iftar dinners picked them up one by one and held them to their ears and tapped them with their fingertips and listened with solemn attention for the precise hollow pitch that promised the sweetest pulp, and above this ancient epicurean ritual, the melon slice of the waning moon slid down the dusty sky.

In such cinnamon dark one night, I stumbled home along the unpaved and unlit Dasht-e-Shor Road with one of my Mazari hosts, the driver who worked for the United Nations. We had just had dinner at the house of his oldest brother, who lived three blocks away. The Taliban had been calling my host's cell phone with death threats all month, but he was in high spirits that evening because the meal had been grand: potato and pumpkin *bolani* and mountains of rice with carrots and raisins and a huge wok of tender goat he had stewed with onions himself, feeding the cooking fire with dry grass that may have come from Oqa and hawking dry spittle on the ground about him for he had not had anything to drink since three-thirty that morning.

During Ramadan, city mullahs made dinner rounds and sat down for iftar with different members of their congregations each night. That night had been the turn of my hosts' oldest brother; the rest of the family had come along as well and brought me with them. The meal had been served in the yard. Because the mullahs were not related to them by blood, the women had to wear headscarves and eat with the children separately from the men, at a *dastarkhan* set on a concrete stoop behind a small copse of poplars and a water tank. And because Ramadan was the month for introspection and piety and the mullahs were supposed to engage the men in a dignified and solemn conversation on divine subjects, the women, even in purdah, had been expected to maintain the formal spirit of the gathering by keeping quiet and not telling jokes.

That imposition itself was enough to send the women into paroxysms of laughter. "These mullahs are like the Taliban," one of the women whispered, and instantly someone squirted chilled Sprite through her nose trying not to crack up, and that foolishness in turn set off a new round of barely controllable giggles that turned to hiccups when someone threw in a racy quip as she reached for *bolani*. I did not understand most of the jokes, but the sniggering they prompted was contagious. We would regain composure and then start laughing again despite ourselves, and we would try to hush one another by slapping one another on the lips and on the thighs, and that was funnier still, and then somebody's baby would crawl into a pool of melon juice and splash it on everyone, and that was slapstick, that was downright hilarious, and mostly we laughed because it felt good to be alive, to eat stewed goat and ignore the stuck-up mullahs, to be together, to be hot, to drink at last under the stars.

Satiated and relaxed on the walk home along the rows of melon vendors, I asked my companion what he had wanted to become when he was a little boy. He and I were almost the same age, and both of us had been children under communism: he, at Bagram Airport outside Kabul, where his father had served as a political officer during the Khalq rule and the Soviet occupation, and I, in Soviet Leningrad, where my parents had been disenfranchised, quasi-dissident intelligentsia.

"I wanted to be a pilot," said my friend. I tripped on an invisible pothole, and he caught me by the elbow.

"I really wanted to be a pilot." His voice was suddenly so lonesome, so earnest, almost begging. I wanted to give him a hug. "But then there was fighting, fighting, fighting. I became a driver."

Our footsteps scraped on the gravel.

"Now I am a land pilot."

We walked on. The golden fingernail of the Ramadan moon scratched the chamois sky. The last prayer of the night, intricate, gauzy, evanescent, swung the city to sleep like a hammock, and the air around us was cloying and sticky with the juice of melons and the residue of millions of sweet and broken dreams.

~~~~

No melons made it to Oqa, no mullahs came to freeload on the villagers' dinners, and even if they had come, there would have been nothing with which to feed them.

A Turkoman proverb says "If we have rice for dinner, life is good." It had been days since the last time Boston and Thawra had cooked rice. Ramadan fast or not, the villagers were going without. The wells from which they drank were running out of water. The fugitives they harbored were running out of luck. The looms on which they wove were running out of thread.

Why did they stay? Which knots tied them to their faded desert, flattened by pitiless heat that had swallowed the mountains and cut the horizons true like a spirit compass? Inertia? Tradition? Laziness? Fear? Knowledge that nowhere else in Afghanistan was better—or that nowhere else in Afghanistan were they welcome? Baba Nazar could think of one who had broken away: Abed Nazar, his nephew, had joined the army and was fighting in the Kashmund Range, a terraced sierra very far away, maybe a month-long walk from Oqa, in Kunar Province—and how was such emigration any good, especially if the boy, God forbid, got hurt?

The rest just hung on, clung to their misweave of a village like clumps of thistle brush as the fickle and difficult soil eroded from under them grain by grain. Amin Bai commanded his invisible troop and entertained opium addicts in his guestroom. Manon the shopkeeper kept his country store and taught his son literacy in the quieter hours of the day. Even Choreh hung around, despite his promises to join the army or the police in exchange for a steady paycheck and government-paid rehab.

One afternoon Choreh and I were ambling about the village, and he took me to visit Abdul Rashid, the blueskinned heroin addict, the younger brother of Jan Mohammad the wedding chef and the son of the ancient Qul Nazar and Kizil Gul, an asthmatic woman with a face so umbered by the sun and so grotesquely disproportionate it possessed the counterintuitive, primeval beauty of a stone idol. Qul Nazar had been a sharecropper in Khairabad until the Taliban had diverted the water away from the fields of his landlords. After that, there were no more crops to tend, no more work. The family sold their animals and moved to Oqa where Kizil Gul could weave. Except there never seemed to be any money for wool, and the two warped poplar beams of a disassembled loom stood idle in the corner of the family's single-room house in which the woman passed her days wheezing at her wayward son between chores.

"You spend all your money on drugs!" she would yell as she squatted by a ceramic basin and covered the dough she had just finished kneading with a tin plate and a folded-up length of tarp.

"We can't afford it!" And she would reach for the tall stack of mattresses, blankets, and clothes festooned with coins and protective charms and motley strips of cloth that loomed like some dull and ancient treasure in the corner of the house and pick off the top of that pile a grimy green *chapan* coat and throw that on top of the tarp, to help the dough rise.

"If it weren't for you, we'd have had rice for dinner tonight!"

If we have rice for dinner, life is good.

At this point Kizil Gul would gulp for air, hyperventilating, exasperated. Choreh and I had walked into the house in the middle of one such dressing-down, but she paid us no attention. Choreh had heard it all before; everyone in the village had—everyone on Earth had, for mothers of addicts around the world repeated the same lament.

And like all addicted sons around the world, Abdul Rashid avoided looking at his mother. He was squatting five paces away in front of a small uneven cat's-tongue flame from an oil lamp. With his left hand he held over the lamp a strip of tinfoil, and he was looking very intently at the tinfoil. On it sizzled a single black speck of heroin. In his right hand Abdul Rashid held a thin metal pipe, like a drinking straw.

"If I quit this," he said to his mother, never taking his eyes off the narcotic he was cooking, "I will die."

He leaned over and placed the pipe so that one end almost touched the heroin, and wrapped his lips around the other end and inhaled. A thin ribbon of brown smoke rushed from the tinfoil into the pipe. He held his breath. He exhaled. No smoke came out of his broad lips. He had collected kindling in the desert for three days and had earned about four dollars for it in Karaghuzhlah and had spent a dollar on heroin. It would last him less than a week.

He noticed me.

"Can you take me to a clinic?"

Kizil Gul looked up from her cooking. She saw me now.

"Oh, yes. I pray to God that you take him to a clinic," she said.

"Take him to the clinic," said Choreh, and grasped my shoulder really hard. Choreh, with pupils barely visible. Stoned since morning. Was he pleading for Abdul Rashid, or for himself, too—for a hope, perhaps, that a treatment was possible, a cure, a solution, that an escape was not just the fantasy of an addled mind?

But when I called the rehab in Mazar to ask about bringing in a new patient, they said the wait for a bed in the detoxification unit was two months, and when I relayed that to Abdul Rashid and Choreh and Amin Bai, the men clicked their tongues and shook their heads, and Amin Bai said: "I can't predict what will happen in two months. I can't predict what is going to happen even tomorrow!"

No one could plan that far ahead in Oqa, so parlously poised between the ancient and the modern, between the world in which artisans hand-carved wooden doors and the world in which these wooden doors were thrust under car tires, between the world of bartered calligonum and the world of two-gigabyte cell phone SIM cards. This village where time at once stood still and slipped by too swiftly to take measure of it, incalculate and unreliable like sand, like atomized grief itself—no one, except for the weavers of carpets.

"One meter left," Thawra said, without looking up. Exhausted. In pain. Her voice so quiet. Probably wishing for the opiate relief her husband and father-in-law had forbidden her.

The two men were leaning into the loom room now, appraising her work.

"It may be finished in twenty, twenty-five days," Amanullah thought out loud.

"I think she'll be done in a month," Baba Nazar agreed. "I'll sell it to a dealer in Dawlatabad or Mazar—whoever will take it." The year before he had sold Thawra's carpet for almost four hundred dollars. But that carpet had been twice as wide. The hunter's lips moved as he worked out the figures in silence. Then he pulled out his ultimate bargaining chip, the one he would offer the merchant to drive up the price, and tried it out on his son, his daughter-in-law, me, the three wobbly chickens that stirred in their down atop the bottom of the carpet.

"It's hard to follow the design."

Amanullah studied his wife then. Her bony arms bare from the elbows down, no jewelry apart from the single silver and garnet ring she had traded from me for a hematite bracelet. He shook his head and walked out of the room, preoccupied.

That evening on our way to the city, Qasim and I drove Amanullah out to the desert where he had left his camels to graze. The plain dry and lifeless. The camels slow in the heat. Amanullah turned in the passenger seat.

"Anna, do you think my wife is too skinny?" he asked. "I told her to stop weaving because she's too thin. I worry about her. That's why she sometimes weaves and sometimes doesn't. So it'll take her a long time. She won't be finished in twenty days."

Then he looked past me, looked at his tiny pale village through the dust-smeared rear window of the taxicab.

"Is this a place worth living?" he said. "The one thing it's got going for it is that it's safe. We are too far from everything to be remembered. No one from outside comes here."

Once during Ramadan, Amanullah called me at dawn and said he was in a *zaranj* headed to Mazar-e-Sharif. We agreed to meet outside the Blue Mosque's north gate. Two hours later from the backseat of Qasim's taxi, I watched my friend pick his uncertain way through a crowd made up mostly of village daytrippers like him, or else immigrants from distant hamlets looking for city work, nameless contributors to the world's latest great migration, the largest population shift in human history. That year population experts in the West were predicting that within a century villages like Oqa would disappear, eroded by depravity and privation, dismantled by the globalized pull of modernity. Metropolises would be full of men like Amanullah, seduced into urban living, bewildered by the sweaty chaos of one another's bodies, humbled by the sparkling blues of the old shrine, confused by the jumble of traffic, shrunken by the awesome speed and volume of the city. There among these selfsame nomads and farmers walked Amanullah, his face pained, haggard, his shoulders drawn, the familiar swing gone from his arms. His strabismus a grimace of suffering. Then he spotted my car and got into the seat next to Qasim and spread his shoulders and stretched out his legs and smiled. Safe again.

We drove around. We drove to a public garden that had a Ferris wheel and two carousels and trampled hard grass behind an iron palisade. The gate was locked. We drove to the hills south of the city and got out of the car and from a dirt road watched the city choke on her own thirsty smog. We drove back into the city and drove to the bazaar, and Amanullah bought shampoo from a stall sticky with last night's melon juice. Then he announced that the city had worn him out, and he farewelled us and left in another *zaranj* for Oqa to watch Thawra's belly round out a little more each day under that shapeless calico dress, the rest of her still fishbone-thin, and to watch her carpet inch, knot by knot, *thk, thk, thk,* toward the top beam of her loom, toward completion, toward the chance of another winter not so hungry.

THE BLIZZARD

The drought broke on Eid al-Adha: the Festival of Sacrifice, Islam's most beloved celebration, which salutes the devotion of Abraham and marks the end of the hajj. Cloudfuls of snow emptied onto the vineyards of Shomali and on the Hindu Kush and on the parched Bactrian plains and on the grainy immensity of Dasht-e-Leili. In Kabul each morning for a week, giant white flakes folded out of a purple predawn sky during the four-thirty prayer as if beckoned down by a muezzin's serenade to rest upon pushcarts abandoned in the frozen brown street mud the night before, upon a little beggar girl in a bloodred dress, upon men cocooned in camelwool blankets slushing to open their shops, upon a boy in a soiled parka riding a donkey bareback and barefoot with his nose running and his mouth open spookily and full of chewed-up straw. The mountains that ranged between the capital and the Khorasan turned completely white like the crimped linen of some ancient god who had risen hastily and left his Cretaceous bed unmade.

Through a pale yellow patina of late-morning clouds and smog, a tentative sun spotlighted islands of brilliant snow on pushcarts and windowsills and flat rooftops. The whole of Kabul Valley was a crinkled primed canvas, and it was impossible to tell where the

mountains ended and the clouds began. Hard rock withered into vapor, and more vapor issued from the lips and lids of crockery and plastic ewers for washing and cups of green tea and from the labyrinthine nostrils of downcast pack animals. The capital breathed outside time and smelled forever of onions and lamb grease and juniper roots that burned in the rusty *bukhari* stoves of its residents.

The latticed marble grave of Babur, the first Mughal emperor, presided over this etched monochrome from the large terraced garden the king himself had helped build in the sixteenth century to cascade to the Kabul River. Babur, né Zahiruddin Muhammad of Fergana, descendant of both Genghis Khan and Tamerlane, was a refined connoisseur of beauty who occasionally ordered his enemies impaled and burned and skinned alive. It was he who exported to India from his beloved Kabul both the luxurious carpets and the art of weaving them. Above Babur Gardens, the vermiform old city wall that outlined the capital's southern boundary ran from Mount Shir Darwazah to the fifth-century stone bulwarks of Bala Hissar, an Afghan army garrison, the symbol of bygone Afghan might, its tortured masonry gray and gagged with snow. Within these twenty-foot walls in 1832, the Afghan emir Dost Mohammad made fateful friends with the British political agent Alexander Burnes. The two had talked, according to the historian Peter Hopkirk, "cross-legged together on a carpet in a room otherwise devoid of furniture." Not fifty years later, the British, by then almost unanimously reviled in Afghanistan, erected inside the fort what one officer described as "a long grim row of gallows," on which they hanged nearly a hundred Afghan men for insurrection.

Downhill from Bala Hissar, Kabul's largest cemetery opened like a white-gloved palm toward the city's largest livestock market. Halfway to it, near the hexagonal black-and-white and graffitied marble grave of the 1970s crooner Ahmad Zahir, a housewife had strung a clothesline from a pear tree to a mausoleum. Copper and red dresses and blue cotton underpants waved at all the dead like a more practical rendition of flags on a martyr's grave. One woman's unsubtle rebuke to her violent world. The sheep and goats and cows below the cemetery lowed and bleated softly and stomped in frozen dirt and farther downhill from the animals a construction market stretched its palisades of debarked poplar beams and bamboo rods along a road that flowed with the shin-deep slush of cemetery snowmelt and livestock refuse all the way north to Ghazi Stadium. Amanullah Khan, Afghanistan's westernizing king who was named *ghazi*—hero—for securing his country's independence from the British in 1919, built the stadium in 1923; in the 1990s, the Taliban used its pitch to carry out public executions of the corrupt and the unchaste. North of the stadium, across the Kabul

River that here dwindled to a thin green stream confined in banks of trash, lay Kabul Wa Nangarhar Street, the beginning of Highway A1—the Grand Trunk Road that connected Kabul to Jalalabad in Nangarhar Province, to Peshawar in Pakistan, to West Bengal in India, and ended in Chittagong, Bangladesh. Most carpets that left Afghanistan in the early twenty-first century—Thawra's carpet possibly among them—traveled out of the country on this road.

The road between Nangarhar and Kabul is tortuous and bad: there are three or four places with very, very narrow passes, and two or three areas with defiles. The Khirilji and Afghans, all of whom are highway robbers, made the road unsafe," Babur wrote in *The Baburnama*, the first true autobiography in Islamic literature. (He composed it in Chagatai Turkic, the extinct language of the statesman-poet Alisher Nava'i, whose work the great Padishah had read during his conquest of Herat in 1506.) Five centuries later the road was a meandering and suppurating lesion ninety-five miles long. Where did the chronicle of iniquities writ upon it begin to unscroll? At Ghazi Stadium, where athletes once again kicked soccer balls on astroturf spread over the old pitch so blood-soaked from executions that it was said grass wouldn't grow on it? Or in Khurd Kabul, now the bland and barren badlands of car mechanics' tin shacks, where in January of 1842 the future emir Wazir Akbar Khan had orchestrated the ambush and slaughter of sixteen thousand British soldiers and camp followers? Engine oil and gasoline and brown snow seeped into the soil to mingle with their remains.

Two Black Hawk helicopters hovered over that old bone- yard and then nuzzled down, down the Kabul River gorge. Down to where the road wound past charred and blis- tered and mangled oil tank-  ers and NATO supply trucks incinerated in recent months by the mortars and rockets of the Taliban. Their debris had been pushed off the road and onto narrow shoulders to rest against the brown and black scarps of igneous rock tagged MOC and OMAR by the sap- pers of Mine Ordnance Clearance and the Organization for Mine Clearance and Afghan Rehabilitation, who in earlier decades had tried to tweeze out of the cuestas the land mines planted during the war with the Soviets. The helicopters disappeared. The hazel river curved and twisted and thrust onto the steep clint banks shoulder- high heaps of detergent foam. Just before Tangi Mahi Par—the Gorge of Fish Scales—a single aspen and some willows flashed gold and silver, and a banner stretched over the two asphalt lanes bid, in English, GOOD-BYE.

For months I had tried to journey down this road in a truck that carried carpets to Pakistan. No truck driver would take me. Expla- nations were many: the road was unsafe for me and the drivers did not want to be responsible for my life; a female passenger, even one in a burqa, would attract attention and make the road unsafe for them; they did not intend to pay export duties on their cargo and worried that I might rat them out. I ended up traveling the carpet route without carpets, in an old Mercedes sedan with Zubair and

Isan, two young Kabuli men who were close friends and made the trip frequently to visit relatives in Peshawar. We left Kabul in late morning because trucks were not allowed to enter the capital past sunrise, which meant that later in the day there were fewer NATO supply trucks on the highway. NATO supply trucks on this stretch of the Grand Trunk Road tended to blow up.

We drove past Ghazi Stadium and through Khurd Kabul and down the mountains past brown Kuchi tents anchored alongside the Kabul River that looked like ancient and wise simurgh birds resting with outstretched wings. Past listing flagpoles aflutter with strips of gold and pink and green and purple cloth that canted out of merestones, mementos of some nameless pilgrims who now were remembered only by their deaths on this road. Past two men asleep on a gryke covered with a straw mat, in the shadow of a tractor-trailer that idled on the shoulder. Through an enfilade of coulees that the river had whittled out in a succession of strange and sinister shapes, some of which ran so narrow and deep that even with the November sun near zenith you could not see the stream. Then the rims of the escarpment parted again. In the dark gulley below, a harrier swooped over argent fields of cauliflower.

At Surobi, a town of rifted rimland commanded that year mostly by the powerful and megalomaniac insurgent chieftain Gulbuddin Hekmatyar, the gorge broadened into a wide valley to make room for the Panjshir River to join the Kabul, and all that water stilled before a hydroelectric dam into a mirror of blue. Tiny fingerlike streams rimmed with yellowing poplars combed through quilted fields of potato and cabbage and winter wheat. The town itself clasped on to granite and marl at an elevation nearly three thousand feet lower than the capital's. Snow had not reached here; it rarely did. On the high south bank of the dammed river, mortars sandbagged on the watchtowers of an Afghan army outpost pointed at a lavender comb ridge across the valley. At the town bazaar, pomegranates sat in cannonball piles beneath sparkling scarves for women and bolts of brown corduroy for men's winter *shalwar kameez* and plastic window sheeting. Three or four men leaned out of the rolled-down windows of two pickup trucks and shucked sunflower seeds and spat the shells upon the ground. They were waiting for a busload of Surobi pilgrims scheduled to return from the hajj that afternoon and had bedecked their trucks with garlands of fluorescent plastic flowers in celebration. They watched with stony faces a caravan of eighteen-wheelers loaded with armored Humvees as it chugged uphill, toward Kabul, past the spot where in November of 2001 a group of gunmen had ambushed four Western journalists riding in a convoy, ordered them out of their cars, and shot them dead. Their blood, too, absorbed by the road that knew no heartsink. On a switchback beside a Soviet T-52 tank mounted on a stone pedestal—a celebration of whose bloody victory, whose decimation?—three boys stood holding leis of fresh-caught carp for sale. Their eyes impassive. They had been standing there forever.

The road narrowed again, rushing east, downhill. There were signs, in Pashto and English. SHALA KAMAR. MOHAMMAD ALI KAS. KA KAS. More tiny settlements along the river road, safeguarding more unnamed bloody memories. The mountains flattened out, their shadowfolds softened, the silty river running through them widened and slowed down once more, flanked now by low ribbonlike escarpments on the north side and tamarisk and saxaul groves to the south. At a speed bump fashioned from a tank tread and a length of rope, a handful of old men chewed their gums and collected alms for the construction of a mosque. At Khairo Khel the river split briefly into several sashaying streams, then pooled again. Black-and-white Kunari cows grazed on feldspar banks and bougainvillaea gushed bright pink from the mud walls of compounds. Sun beat through the car windows. We took off our sweaters.

Near the Darunta Dam, which the Soviets had built outside Jalalabad in the 1960s, the road ducked into a tunnel and emerged inside an emerald city. Vines climbed up and down date palms and swung from tamarisks and pines. In the clearings, boys who were wealthy enough not to have to work played cricket on lawns. Men napped on charpoy beds beneath eucalyptus trees, and the pieced green sunlight rebated from the mirrors sewn into their skullcaps and vests. Water buffalo in their ancient indigo skin waded through paddies of sugarcane, and children thrust plastic bags of chopped cane into the windows of cars stuck in traffic jams at intersections that suffocated with exhaust from all manner of trucks—pug-nosed pre–World War II Bedfords, fifty-year-old Volvos, Soviet Kamazes, all bejeweled with elephantine carcanets and torsades the width of a human thigh and braided tow chains, and painted with pointillist swans and waterfalls and sun-drenched pastorals and doe-eyed maidens and turbaned horsemen ascending turquoise and fuchsia mountains on white stallions.

"Maybe some carpets in these," Zubair said.

"Maybe opium," Isan responded.

. . .

The Torkham border crossing between Afghanistan and Pakistan lay fifty tamarisk-lined miles east of Jalalabad. The smoggy Spin Ghar Range friezed the valley. To the east lay the entrance to the Khyber Pass—Kipling's "sword cut through the mountains," or, in the words of the American traveler-journalist Lowell Thomas, "the funnel through which India's ravishers have poured ever since history began," though, in fact, many conquerors of India had preferred, like Alexander the Great, the more manageable albeit more circuitous southern routes until Babur's grandson Akbar built the first road through the Khyber Pass in 1581. Thomas journeyed

through the pass in 1922, three years after Afghan independence, which the British border guards on the eastern side of the border, in Khyber Pakhtunkhwa on India's North-West Frontier, observed by planting a sign that proclaimed: IT IS ABSOLUTELY FORBIDDEN TO CROSS THIS BORDER INTO AFGHAN TERRITORY.

The border crossing on the Afghan side was grimy and cluttered, and sprawled for miles. It offered everything and nothing, the way borders do: cheap nylon prayer rugs and counterfeit alcohol, pyramids of apples white with road dust and stacked directly on the ground upon black veins of engine oil and pyramids of soda cans stacked on plywood shelves next to ghetto blasters pumping out Hindi pop, auto parts new and wrested out of cars lost to unmentioned accidents. Cliques of stubbled taxi drivers with sour breath called, "To Jalalabad—to Jalalabad—to Jalalabad—to Jalalabad!" There were women in burqas and high heels, and women in dark embroidered veils and many layers of mirrored and laced Kuchi skirts, and matrons in long beige headscarves that trailed on the ground, and there was one woman in skinny jeans and knee-high high-heeled boots and a stiff perm. Sooty lace bras for sale lay on display on patches of gravel, and cattle and some camels grazed on petrol-soaked grass slow and oblivious because animals know no abstract boundaries drawn by men. Coteries of American soldiers in body armor and with rifles at the ready surveyed pilgrims from behind reflective sunglasses, and some of them stopped male pedestrians and scanned their retinae with handheld contraptions that looked like cell phones. Boys with angry jaws zigzagged in sandals or barefoot through the crowd and pushed low wooden and metal wheelbarrows loaded with vegetables, or with blackened and moldy palms of tiny Jalalabad bananas, or with old men or women of all ages with and without infants who crouched on thin mattresses thrown on the bottoms of the carts; and whole families inched on foot toward the border crossing, toward the promise of medical treatment or reunion or comfort or simply of something other than this, other than Afghanistan—for above all else, this frontier, like most frontiers in the world, offered promises, promises often inarticulate and distorted, shiny and improbable baubles, hopes of respite from war and disease, half-clandestine and barely contained expectations of sudden and semilicit enrichment, possibilities of journeys taken and not taken, of journeys taken in dreams only, journeys that have turned or would yet turn to nightmares. Promises hung over the Khyber Pass so thick they obfuscated and warped the very nature of the border itself, and if everybody's eyes watered, it was from the density of chance and hope and desire in the air as much as from the soot and diesel fumes disgorged by scores and scores of trucks.

The trucks idled on road shoulders for almost a mile in ranks of three and four in both directions. During the day, the border was open for pedestrian traffic only; the trucks crossed only at night; no other vehicles were allowed across. On the northern shoulder of the road, facing west, a convoy of twenty or thirty oil tankers that had crossed from Pakistan at night was getting ready to pull out toward Kabul that afternoon. Cross-legged on top of each tanker sat a man, a sentry on the suicide mission to watch the mountains for terrorists once the convoy began to move.

"And if he sees someone?"

"Then he bangs on the tanker and maybe the driver hears the banging."

"And then what?"

Zubair shrugged.

"Nothing. These men on top are going to be the first to die."

On the southern shoulder of the road, the Volvos and the Kamazes and the Bedfords stood mostly cargoless. Two hundred of them, maybe three, waiting for the border crossing to open for truck traffic. Their drivers sat in the cabins or squatted in the shade of the massive tires or stood smoking cigarettes with other drivers or slept atop the trailers. We walked the length of the line bound for Pakistan twice and asked all the awake drivers we saw whether they were carrying carpets. No luck.

In an air-conditioned room that smelled like chocolate, an Afghan customs press officer said eight or ten trucks that carried carpets passed through his border each month. Each paid a five-dollar processing fee to customs, plus a tax that equaled two percent of the carpets' estimated worth. The tax, the officer explained, was a mandatory charitable donation to the Red Crescent. He spat on his fingers and separated a blank sheet of letter paper from a stack and wrote: "5 $ USD" and, below it, "2 %." He underscored both lines twice, handed the paper to me, and turned to a petitioner in a black striped suit at his desk. "Go away," the press officer said. "And next time do not come back without a present."

A fifteen-foot concrete blast wall surrounded the customs building and a conglomeration of metal containers next to it. Each of those also was individually bunkered behind concrete barriers and giant sandbags. The containers belonged to American soldiers. Latter-day centurions embattled at the gateway to a restive province that was slipping away from them the way it had slipped away from legionnaires for generations. A concrete wall in front of one container was stenciled with quasi-Gothic black letters that spelled THE CASTLE. I stopped a sergeant with the taro-leaf shoulder patch of the Twenty-fifth Infantry Division, stationed in Hawaii. The sergeant's name tag read: STORY. His face was hidden behind his sunglasses and his helmet and the helmet's chinstrap. Our conversation was brief.

"Haven't seen any carpets," he said. "Anything else I can do for you, ma'am?"

And he walked away.

~~~~

We spent that night in Jalalabad, at the house of Isan's uncle. The uncle lived near a small bazaar with his two wives and the several wives of his brothers, who were businessmen and spent most of their time on the road. Through the heavy living room curtain we could hear the patio tiles ring with the bare feet of the women and their many children, with the clank of aluminum washbasins, with splashes of water that ran from a single brass spout. The children peeked into the living room and whispered to one another, and after a while, some of them came in and perched on mattresses in the corner farthest away from me and the men—except for a bold ten-year-old girl named Kamrana. Kamrana sat next to me and spoke to me in Farsi and sign language, and drew elephants and princesses in my notepad. The princesses had long eyelashes and heart-shaped lips.

After sundown, the men and I dined on rice and okra and chicken, and Isan's uncle told me the story of his life, a life of crossing the border again and again as war came and went from his city. He asked me about my life of crossing borders and tramping through wars. He asked me about life in America. He said: "I have a brother. He has been living in America for fifty-six years. I wrote him a long letter, and instead of writing me back, he called me and said: 'I don't have the time to read this. Why don't you just summarize? You should just get to the main point.'

"Why is that?" my host asked. "Why do people in America have no time to read long letters?"

Kamrana cleared away the dinner platters and brought green tea and hot sweetened milk boiled with walnuts. The dim air in the room became scented with cardamom.

After dinner, the uncle and my companions remained in the living room to smoke cigarettes and sleep on mattresses arranged along the walls, and I joined the women and children who crowded for warmth into a single bedroom. We slept fully clothed under Chinese polyester blankets on thin bedrolls laid on the floor side by side in an interlocking mosaic, and we held hands through the night in an astonishing act of faith, as though the mortises and tenons of our linked fingers, our elemental intimacy, could grant us sanctuary against war. Our breath synchronized. I remembered another night of such communal ritual, in Karima's home in Andkhoi, and my heart swelled. Then I remembered that six months earlier and less than two miles away American soldiers had shot and killed a girl like Kamrana when that girl had been sleeping in her uncle's house. Whose hand had she been holding that night? I felt for Kamrana's pulse in her slack fingertips—one, two, three, *thk, thk, thk*—and I felt against it the beat of my own slower heart that pushed and pushed tenderness and heartbreak together through my bloodstream.

⌇⌇⌇

The premature winter locked away the Khorasan behind its many cold latches of seclusion. Ice crusted mountain passes. Weather delayed planes. The galleries of Salang were snowed in, and motorists on either side of the tunnel idled in frozen smog for days, dancing little shivering stomps next to their taxis and buses and semis and blowing into their cold-raw hands, appointments broken, hospital visits delayed, carpets uncollected and undelivered.

In the afternoon of the first day of Eid, nearly a meter of snow dumped unexpectedly and almost all at once onto the Bactrian plains. In Karaghuzhlah, a hundred and twenty of the thousand sheep the boys had taken out to pasture that morning got stuck in the drifts and froze to death. The snow melted and fell again and melted again. The snow turned to rain. Great legatos of rain stroked the desert by day, and by night the thinnest membrane of ice shingled the waterlogged wastes. The soggy loess became the color and consistency of a chunk of chocolate melting in a pot, a hard and slippery clay bed coated with three or four inches of viscous and velvety muck that extended to the rim of the world. White flashes of unpicked cotton interrupted the expanse of brown. The eroded adobe of the city walls of Balkh sagged under the rain, and beneath these walls murders of crows sailed over pale green fields of waxlike cauliflower. The shunpike to Asfakhan Shrine sloshed unused through dormant fields, and in the ruts grooved out by mad pilgrims' buses gossamer ice shone like mica. Beneath the snowcapped minaret of Zadyan, Zarifshah Bibi, Baba Nazar's mine-crippled daughter, was trapped indoors for days because her prosthesis was of no use in the slush. Unseen in the desert, POMZ-2M fragmentation mines, these afterbirths of the war against the Soviets, shifted loose in their pulpy soil like sinister corncobs, each a latent wound, a time warp waiting to collect a ghastly oblation of limbs from some child or shepherd or farmer not yet born at the time of its emplacement. In Siogert, two long resilient white spills of unmelted snow stared up at the eggshell sky from the spot on the road where in October local vigilantes had killed two Taliban scouts. Or maybe it was where the village teacher had been killed that spring. The weather treated all blood equally. The road was mucoid, and days and days went by when no transport or man or beast traveled on it.

The Khorasan was shutting down and shutting itself off—for the winter, or a year, or a century. Each village, each hamlet on the plains, was on its own now, fenced off from the rest of the world by sodden land, alone with its history, its anguish, its singular beauty.

Only Dasht-e-Leili in the west never slaked its thirst and spun its sand into yellow and dense *tufans* beneath the pillowy low sky as it always had. Smudged by these storms to the point of seeming incorporeal, stern men draped with bright garlands of plastic flowers that clashed absurdly with their mud-splattered brown *shalwar kameez* waited outside roadside mosques for returning hajjis in stoic silence like ghosts ordered eons ago into ceremonious and grave line formations.

The storms had washed Mazar-e-Sharif like a body for burial. Pale sepulchral sun filtered through fogging slush and stove smoke, and everywhere the gutters oozed with melting snow mixed with black sludge, the blood of sacrificial animals, old grudges, millennial regrets. Sheepskins hung to dry on mud fences slowly rotted. The stoops and storefronts of Mazar's Dasht-e-Shor neighborhood where I was staying had emptied of the men who in warmer weather would spend afternoons squatting in semicircles in thin strips of shade or else hold on to one another's handshakes near water pumps for hours and gossip and slaver over the ankles of the veiled women who passed by.

My hosts' compound also grew quieter, more somber, that winter. Worn out by Taliban threats that had hounded him all summer, one of the brothers, the one who had been a driver for the United Nations, had fled to Tajikistan soon after Ramadan with his pregnant wife and children. Another, a young unmarried journalist, had fled to Europe and sought political asylum in Scandinavia. Orphaned this way at once of two sons and three grandchildren, her arthritis amplified by the cold, Dear Mother the matriarch sighed deeper and prayed more often and locked herself for hours in her widow's quarters at the front of the house. The electric water pump below the cement courtyard froze and broke, and the large family washed from batteries of plastic ewers in unheated bathrooms that reeked of unflushed toilets. When they bathed, the brothers who remained in the house sang melancholy love songs, beautifully and in tune, but their voices were muffled by the quilts that hung from bedroom doorframes and window sashes to trap warm air, because *bukhari* heat tended to draft out through the cracks as soon as the fire went out. The long hallways stood freezing and empty and dark. On a trellis by the garbage heap a single clematis blossom clung to the vine, a dying purple flame preserved in verglas. In the blue pre-dawn, muezzins' four-o'clock arpeggios clinked through the blanketed windows like distant icicles breaking.

On a drizzly morning, I slogged down Dasht-e-Shor Street to the twin domes of the Blue Mosque. Schoolgirls in black uniforms leaned into a stiff wind that blew frigid mist past enormous fields of refuse. The street was a river of gunge through which men on bicycles and women in galoshes skidded in slow motion, trying to keep upright in the mud. At the southern tip of that foul thoroughfare, the shrine glittered in the morning fog as though encased in ice, so unsoiled it seemed a thing separate from that city, an attestation to some virtue contained within. Men shuffled in reverent quietude past the snowflake-white doves that roosted in the thousands atop its spiral minarets and in the vaulted arch of its mihrab, and drew their *patu* blankets over their heads and around their shoulders, and in the early-morning cold, the condensation from their breath collected on their beards like tinsel. Pilgrims in search of sanctuary and comfort. Over the years I had been one of them several times and here I was again.

Worshippers left their shoes heavy with cold mud at the east gate that led to the mosque's inner yard, and walked across the tiles of white and black marble in stocking feet and entered the shrine. The cold from the tiles bored into their soles. Which invocations did they whisper inside? Which millennial transgressions did they ask to right? The tiles ricocheted with the sharp applause of the pigeons' flutter, the same indifferent ovation for generations of pilgrims, winter after winter, war after war.

An old man was selling pewter platefuls of millet seed to feed the pigeons. I bought one. Ten minutes of bliss for ten afghanis, about twenty cents. The birds alighted on my head, shoulders, arms, hands; they walked over my feet. I thought: flying must feel like this. I thought my heart would burst. Then I started laughing. I stood in the middle of a war zone, draped in fluttering white birds, and laughed and laughed. A few dozen yards away, a girl tossed bits of stale bread in the air and the pigeons pirouetted, collided with one another in bursts of impossible whiteness, dove down to catch the crumbs. The girl was laughing, too. A Mazari journalist once told me: "The West is all about technology. The East is all about the mystical." He had been drinking bootleg vodka he had hidden in a plastic bag because drinking alcohol in Afghanistan carried the punishment of imprisonment or lashing, and he was not so much mystical as just plain drunk. But I thought of his words among the solace of the pigeons of the Blue Mosque. I knew then that the birds were there to keep us sane, buoyed, somehow, through the extreme blue solitudes of winter and wartime.

That evening, over a dinner of bread and *lobio* and stewed cauliflower, I asked one of my hosts if I could take his daughter Lena to the shrine with me someday to feed the pigeons. Lena was ten and had thick braids; and she liked to come into my room to teach me a word or two of Farsi sometimes, or sometimes to insist that I kiss the fat and milky cheek of her baby brother, whom she carried on her hip, or sometimes to give me a quick hug and run away. I was very fond of her. But sometimes she would come in, lipsticked and with her hair undone and carrying a little portable radio so that she could dance before me, and seeing her walk through the door with that radio terrified me because I knew how that dance ended. It ended with her going down on her knees in front of me. There at my feet the ten-year-old girl would close her eyes and quake and ripple her shoulders and gyrate her still-flat chest in the smooth and knowing way of a very grown woman, a way that reached into some forbidden and unnamable darkness inside me and made me absolutely, utterly afraid.

Lena's father said she could not go with me to feed the white birds. He said it was too cold and her feet would get wet. He said she only had one pair of shoes, her brother's Chinese sneakers. It would take ages for them to dry in that cold.

❯❯❯

In that tapestry of isolation, Oqa's was the most inviolable.

The village was sequestered behind incalculable acreages of muck. Impounded in this bone-clasping cold beneath a corrugated sky in which no sun or moon or stars any longer appeared. Unattainable, unreachable, hermetic. Fall was hunting season, and hundreds of ducks labored southward between the brown-gray desert and the brown-gray clouds, yet Baba Nazar could not leave the hummock to hunt. Ismatullah and Ozyr Khul could not wander the dunes in search of calligonum to trade for rice and oil. Manon the shopkeeper could not bring in fresh supplies of Crown safety razor blades and Pine cigarettes. The Oqans had reassembled the *bukhari* stoves they had stashed away for the summer and fed them frugal handfuls of dried grass and huddled around them refilling and refilling and refilling their chipped teacups with murky hot well water from soot-blackened pitchers. Even the camels stayed put, hitched to corroded antiaircraft shell casings driven into the slippery trampled-down clay, or else corralled behind ephemeral enclosures of thistle they slowly chewed out of the walls.

"When are you coming, Anna?" Amanullah demanded over the phone. "Everyone misses you. Our village is sometimes okay, and sometimes not good. There are always rumors that there are Taliban. But we are the same people you know, and we love you."

Tenderness spilled through my abdomen and down my arms, and my fingertips felt warm for the first time in days. I pictured Thawra's weaving hands eaten raw by the weather under her improbable thistle roof. Then Amin Bai took the cell phone from Amanullah and said there was no road to come on and told me to wait for the rain to abate.

Two weeks would pass before anyone could leave or enter Oqa.

That night I wore two sweaters over two pairs of *shalwar kameez* and slept poorly under a heavy polyester blanket and a sheepskin coat, and when I did sleep I had a neverending nightmare. In it, my laptop, my notebooks, my pens were all washed away by a flood, vanished in an umber gruel that had come from all directions.

~~~

S ee this corner? In the time of the Taliban they hanged a young man in this place."

"See this shrine? Seven brothers were killed here. They were Uzbek. They were fleeing the Taliban, in 1997. We were all fleeing then."

"See this flag? One brother killed another brother here over land. It was after the fall of the Taliban. Then someone killed the killer; I'm not sure who."

"See this poplar grove? There was a bloody fight between the mujaheddin and the Pashtuns here, in the second year of the Taliban's rule. It went on for days."

"See this crater? A Talib on a bicycle blew up here and killed a storekeeper before Nawruz. I was at a café down the block, finishing my lunch."

"Anna! See this?"

Mnemonics of gore charted young Qasim's world. See what now? What was I looking at? The frosted jags of the Hindu Kush against the cold blush of dawn. A golden eagle lifting up heavily from a limestone outcrop to hunt for breakfast. The taxi driver saw a crime scene. He said: "There was a mullah five years ago, Mullah Ghafur. He was Baluch, from Karaghuzhlah. A man called Shir killed him. I think it was over money. Shir was Uzbek."

Another bloody knot on the loom of the Khorasan, where war was one of the weavers. Its sickle went *clack clack clack*, like the rattling of dry bones.

Whom to blame for the unhealed scar tissue of fratricidal violence that blemished this terrain indelibly, irredeemably, conditioning people's memories and yearnings? The Pashtun Taliban who had mutilated, shot, and slit the throats of some six thousand Hazara in Balkh in 1998? The Hazara and Uzbek militiamen who had joined forces to slaughter three thousand Pashtun Taliban soldiers the year before? Or the perpetrators of the smaller, village-scale genocides—the Hazara who had supposedly killed twenty-two Pashtuns from Shingilabad the year before the Taliban took power; their Pashtun neighbors who had ostensibly murdered five Hazara from Karaghuzhlah around the same time? The strips of colorful cloth that whiffled from knobbly wooden poles over their graves a decade and a half later were mnemonics for the scores that never seemed to be settled. What about, then, King Abdur Rahman, whose genocidal unification campaign forcibly resettled ten thousand rebellious Ghilzai Pashtun families to this high desert from their ancestral lands south of the Hindu Kush in the 1890s, diluting the tribal structures of the disloyal Pashtuns and weakening the bastion of the other minorities?

Perhaps the violence was a constant replay, a caroming echo of much earlier wars. A limbic memory of some unresolved skirmish between a common ancestor of the Hazara and Uzbeks, who carried the Y chromosome of Genghis Khan, and an antecedent of the Tajiks and Pashtuns and Turkomans, whose haplogroup possibly had been pushed to the Khorasan out of somewhere in modern-

day Ukraine by the last glaciation. Or older still, of Cain and Abel arguing in the Great Rift Valley. And maybe it was even older than that, older than our common African ancestors, geomorphic, forged in the tens of millions of years of incessant smashing of the Eurasian plate and the Gondwanaland supercontinent, during a whole era of thrusting and kneading like dough the rock that had made this land.

We had started for Oqa early that morning. The road soaked in blood old and new squished under the tires. In the gullies—"See this, Anna? Taliban killed a teacher from Siogert here, then the villagers killed two Pashtuns in revenge"—snow lay in ultramarine shadows. On the car stereo Shamsuddin Masrur sang about a maiden sweet like a Sistani pomegranate to the lacy twang of a two-stringed *dutar* lute.

"He was from Mazar," Qasim said. "The Taliban shot him in his home because he was a musician. He was an old man then."

Fifteen miles south of Oqa, just past the turnoff to Karaghuzhlah, the tires veered and locked and fistfuls of mud pelted the car windows. The engine muttered and stalled. There was no more road ahead, just a sea of brown muck. Qasim opened his door and tried the surface with his foot. His foot sank to the talus.

"Oqa is closed today," Qasim said. He turned in his seat, beaming. "Let's have lunch at my father's house."

Hassan Khan—warlord, farmer, Qasim's father, Amin Bai's friend, keeper of demoiselle cranes—was in good spirits. He had lost twenty of his ninety sheep in the Eid blizzard, but all the rain and snowmelt promised a plentiful almond harvest next year. When we arrived, he was presiding over a small gathering of male neighbors and relatives in a long narrow guestroom. On the mattress next to Hassan Khan reclined Jan Mohammad, the beautiful warlord whom everyone called Janni and whom I had met at Ozyr Khul's wedding in Oqa. Janni's bodyguards sat or stood by the door; one was feeding the lone *bukhari* that loosed smoke into the room in long opaque scarves. Across the room slumped Hassan Khan's older brother, Rustam Khan, who kept scrapbooks of events and phenomena he considered important—the inauguration of President Hamid Karzai, the electric storm years back during which two villagers died of fright in the desert, the wedding of a neighbor's son and niece, the map of Italy he had drawn and colored by hand. Rustam Khan had a long gray beard and a collection of books he stored under lock and key in a tin chest. The villagers called him the Historian. He chewed opium for his arthritis and often was stoned.

It had begun to rain again. Cold silver needles pricked at the dirt in the courtyard, streaked in quick transparent veins down the glass of the guestroom's sole window. All this water boring through the clay to quench the tree roots in Hassan Khan's almond and apricot orchards. He smiled. The rain and the *bukhari* heat and the presence of guests impelled him to reminisce. Over rice and a dish of fried sheep fat called *jaz*, he recounted fondly the sacking of nearby Pashtun villages after the retreat of the Taliban ten years earlier. He had commanded a troop of a hundred men then, sometimes two hundred. "In Shahrak, in one garden, seventeen of my men were killed in one day. But we won." He said there had been "many Taliban" in those villages then, and that they once again were "full of Taliban."

"What about Karaghuzhlah?"

"No, no Taliban here. The security is good."

"But they were here during Ramadan. Where did they go?"

"There's nothing to worry about, Anna. You're my guest. If you'd like to walk around at night, I can give you a gun."

A helicopter gunship rumbled in the low wet sky above the compound. The rain quieted. My host added, in English: "No problem."

The other men in the room chuckled at that. Rustam Khan reached into his vest pocket and pulled out a folded piece of lined paper and unfolded it and tweezed off with his fingernails a small crumb of black opium resin that was contained within and placed it on his tongue and folded back the package and put it away. Then he closed his eyes and leaned back against the wall.

Janni spoke: "The Taliban elder of Karaghuzhlah, Gul Ahmad, who now calls himself Mullah Zamir, is not here. He is in Pakistan for the winter. When he goes to Pakistan in the winter, the other Taliban also go. When he comes back, next summer, the Taliban will also come back and we'll fight them."

Janni took a drag from a cigarette. He held it between his long

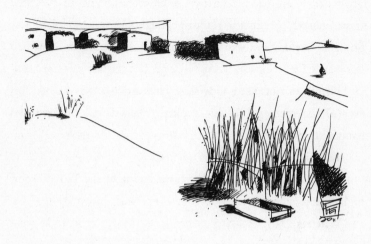

and sensuous middle finger and forefinger, and as he smoked, he held his palm turned up delicately as if receiving some benediction. An exquisite palm. The palm of a killer.

"He goes to Pakistan because his motorcycle doesn't work here in the winter. It gets stuck. In the summer they come with twenty or forty motorcycles and fight with us. Every winter we have peace and every summer we have war."

Janni's bodyguards nodded: yes, yes, the warfare was seasonal, like farmwork. You flooded the paddies for rice in May and you fought. You sowed winter wheat in the fall and then you rested till spring. The cycles of violence were just another timeless way of measuring time in the Khorasan.

"*Pah!*" Hassan Khan exclaimed. "This is not good war. I've seen lots of war. I fought a lot. This is not good war. This is like a dog-fight. People in this war shoot at the sky. They shoot from the sky. They make bombs and leave them to blow one another up. We shot at one another, up close. In Kabul we fought up close, we killed fifty people in one day and watched them die right next to us. Now *that* was war."

Like all warriors since Odysseus, Hassan Khan was trussed forever to the memories of his exploits, defined and inspired and haunted by them.

Suddenly he leaned over the *dastarkhan*.

"Anna! Do you want to go with me and fight the Taliban some night?"

"When?"

"Whenever you want."

"But wait, I thought you said there were no Taliban in your village."

"If we don't find Taliban, we'll just fight Pashtuns," Hassan Khan said. "There's a village, Alozai, they are all Taliban but very weak. We wouldn't fight in the village—we would fight on the road."

At this, Rustam Khan opened his eyes, awakening from an opiate dream.

"All Pashtuns are Taliban," he said. "Their women are Taliban. Their dogs are Taliban. Their donkeys are also Taliban."

The *jaz* was gone and some boys brought in thermoses of green tea and pewter plates of fresh yogurt and some unshucked almonds and Rustam Khan tore off some more opium to chew. For a time we sat without talking, shucking and eating almonds and smoking and sipping tea. After a while, Janni and his bodyguards left; and my hosts' wives and sisters and daughters and aunts filed into the room and squatted and shucked more almonds and drank more tea and made small talk. They talked about the weather. They talked about the children. They talked about the Indian soap opera all the women had liked to watch five years earlier, when for a whole year and for the first time in anyone's life Karaghuzhlah had a powerful village generator that went on from seven until nine at night. They talked about how after a year the village elders had decided that the generator had to go. They talked about the arbitrariness of the powerful and the unavailing and neverending struggles of the weak, about the discrepancy between the rich and the poor and the hypocrisy of the pious, reciting over and over the parables that have been rehashing themselves on every inhabited landmass on Earth since the beginning of time, until there was nothing more to add. A silence fell.

Did I by any chance know, Qasim's teenage sister asked then, shyly, deferentially, what had happened to the Indian family in the soap opera?

It grew dark and a child was sent for a kerosene lamp. An old aunt snoozed against a floor cushion, attended by a girl. Outside the window purple clouds blew low past the Milky Way. In the eighth century less than ten miles to the southwest of Hassan Khan's house, a boy named Jafar ibn Muhammad al Balkhi, later known in the West as Abu Ma'shar, watched the same ever-spiraling galaxy. He would grow up, move to Baghdad, become the preeminent astrologer at the Abbasid court, and compile the *Great Introduction to*

Astrology, an eight-volume text that drew on the philosophy and astrology of pre-Islamic Mesopotamia, India, and Aristotle, and which, translated into Latin in the twelfth and thirteenth centuries, formed the basis of Western scientific astrology.

"Which stories do you tell your children about stars?" I asked the women.

What a silly question. They shook their heads and waved their hands to shoo it away. Golden jewelry shimmered in orange lamplight.

"We are illiterate."

"All we do all day is work with animals."

"We have no time to tell our children about the stars."

I tried again.

"But what were the stories your mothers told you?"

The women laughed.

"Our mothers were the same way. They also had no time."

Hassan Khan began to list the stars of Libra, which had reached its zenith on the first day of Mizan, one month earlier. Zuben al Shamali. Zuben al Genubi. Zuben al Akrab. Beta Librae, Alpha Librae, Gamma Librae. "When I was young, I knew the names of constellations," he said. "But now I forget."

"When Libra first appears, some farmers mate male and female sheep," offered Rustam Khan. He no longer bothered to open his eyes, and he intoned from his corner of the room dappled in leaping lamp shadows like some entranced necromancer. "Some farmers say that when Mars and another star come close together it will rain and snow soon.

"But I don't remember which star it is."

And the Historian retreated into his soporific stupor for the rest of the night and left me to ponder the workings of memory and what it chooses to retain and to leave behind, its capacity to highlight the hurt and eclipse the beauty and alter our perception of time and love and trespass, its profound power to shape and reshape the narrative of its owners' personal and communal past, and so to configure their future. The lamp on the floor flickered and hissed, and outside in the cold and woozy desert the war ebbed and flowed, ebbed and flowed.

～～～

The next day fine and endless rain sieved out of the sky that was white and low and of a piece, and I rented a horse to take me to Oqa. A boy brought it to Hassan Khan's first courtyard where the outhouse stood. It was a draft horse, liver chestnut, and it was saddled with a burlap sack stuffed with straw that was tied to its midsection with rope and a *patu* folded in half was thrown over the sack. The horse had no intention of traveling across the desert in the rain, with or without a rider. It shied when I spoke to it and crabbed sideways when I took hold of the bridle, and when I laid my hand on its muzzle, it bared its teeth and snarled. It threw me the minute I mounted.

Hassan Khan made me stay again for lunch, of course. We sat in his family room on the second floor of his house, and we ate a hot soup of tender lamb and stale bread and raw onions, and then we drank tea with green raisins, tiny bursts of hot summer sun that made me forget my sprained wrist, bruised kidney, the cold outside.

In the wet vines beneath the window a demoiselle crane purred its lonesome song that was as old and as desolate as the rain-veiled peaks of the Hindu Kush, and somewhere a village muezzin chanted about mercy, and compassion, and grace.

‹‹‹‹

The red tractor jerked and pitched with each groove of the November fields, and the slat-board wagon hitched to it with a length of frayed yellow nylon rope wobbled and creaked. In the wagon, held more or less in place by granite drags and lashed to the wooden sideboards like a giant trussed scorpion, lay an enormous plough. In the front of the wagon, in the small space left by the plough, seven passengers crouched in silence, draped in dirty *patus* to keep out the skull-size globs of mud the tractor's immense rear wheels chucked with great accuracy into the wagon bed. Behind this unwieldy train the winter trees of Karaghuzhlah stood inked against a pale yellow firmament. A monotonous nimbostratus beneath which low and massive sudsy clouds rushed eastward like a ghost cavalry unleashed by some jinn of the Occident. Fog rose from a sepia field of unharvested cotton like tufts of cotton itself evaporating into this cold dawn, and by the village walls the fragile green needles of winter wheat were peeking through the mud already, coaxed out by two weeks of rain and snow. In all other directions a flat and trout-colored desert stretched toward the world's rim in a feathering of coral, pale ocher, and blue-gray where the mud reflected the Michelangelo sky. A wet wind blew.

The tractor was a four-wheel-drive, eighty-horsepower giant

made in Soviet Belarus several decades earlier. It weighed four tons. Its rear wheels stood six feet tall. Faded red ribbons streamed from its windshield, to protect from the evil eye its driver and passengers and, most importantly, the engine itself, for this was Karaghuzhlah's sole tractor, the same tractor that had pulled Qasim's taxi out of a dune in Oqa that Ramadan. Now it was taking four day laborers and the plough to work a field about five miles north of the village. The day laborers were Uzbek and had stern, exhausted faces and beards all. The other three passengers in the wagon were Ramin, one of my Mazar hosts, who had come along to translate and for the sake of adventure; Qasim the driver, who had come along because he felt it was his responsibility to follow me even when his taxi could not; and I.

It had been raining for two weeks straight, and there was no telling when it would stop long enough for the desert to become passable by car. Before dawn in the middle of November, Ramin, Qasim, and I went to the bazaar in the city, bought three and a half kilos each of onions and rice and apples, drove to Karaghuzhlah, parked Qasim's taxi by the outhouse in his father's compound, and set out to Oqa across the soggy barrens on foot. I was going to honor Baba Nazar's enduring invitation and spend a night in the village at last.

The land underfoot was scoured smooth and supple like a lover's body. The wind bent the golden organ pipes of dry reeds in the gulches. On the horizon, smoke from shepherds' fires blew like kisses. A golden eagle rose ahead of us and flew low, a swatch of desert picked up by a gust, leading the way over a purple film of withered cousinia. My nylon burqa flapped after it like a flightless blue bird. We were about two miles out of Karaghuzhlah when we heard a rumble behind us: the red tractor was making its way up north. We hitched a ride. A thousand years ago on this stretch of the Great Silk Road pilgrims would fall in with camel caravans this way.

The tractor pulled the wagon north in wrenching spasms. Each time it would arrive at an irrigation ditch, three of the farmhands would jump off, unhitch the wagon, shovel down the canal, and the tractor would run back and forth over it to make the rut more or less level. The workers then would retie the wagon, and onward the tractor would lurch to the next dike, and the next, and the next. In the steamed-up cabin the driver and the navigator sipped green tea from glass cups. We in the wagon held on to the splintery side-boards, to the plough, to one another. The leather armpit of Ramin's jacket was warm against my left knee. Someone warned me to keep my feet close or the plough would cut them clean off. Someone threw a blanket over my head to protect me from the projectile mud, and I struggled from under its wet wool that reeked of ma-nure and sheep fat and woodsmoke, and my burqa came off with it, and then everyone was laughing, laughing.

The tractor stopped in the middle of the desert a third of the way to Oqa: the farmers had arrived. We thanked the driver and farewelled the Uzbeks and walked again. Walked on the Earth's very skin, rose, raw, resonant. It seemed made to be walked, so tem-pered by the feet of numberless generations of wayfarers like us among which now were our own feet. We leaned into the wind, then against it. Three Magi strapped into bags of onions, of apples, of rice. We walked through untilled fields and then through a land that bore no trace of cultivation. Walked on pottery shards, their glaze washed to a shimmer by the rain and blinking up from the ground like splintered memories of clear sky. Walked on sheep crania and spent shell casings and bones of gerbils and maybe land mines and the unseen bones of armies that had been wasted here.

We had walked for two hours, maybe more, when we saw in a muddy esker a young goatherd. He wore an outsize parka, and he was leaning on a walking stick with his left hand and picking his nose with the forefinger of his right. Thirty or forty mud-spattered goats trotted silently about him. The boy regarded our small procession with polite curiosity. He did not move to greet us, not out of unfriendliness but out of the economy that is the parsimonious habit of men who are rewarded poorly for their hard work. Even the youngest men of the desert knew to be frugal with their movement. As we drew closer, he took the finger out of his nose and wiped his nose with the top of his right hand and studied whatever had rubbed off for a second and at last thrust his hand in his pocket.

"Oqa!" the men called out.

"Oqa?"

"Oqa, Oqa!"

"Ah!" The boy pointed northeast.

"May you never grow tired!" The boy pulled his right hand back out of his pocket and raised it halfway to his face, fingers together, the palm facing sideways, in the thrifty blessing of his austere land. In twenty more minutes, first the billowing barchans and then the lone cemetery marker shaped themselves out of the mist, and finally the blind houses themselves, clinging to their infertile rain-darkened hillock and crowned with thin ribbons of *bukhari* smoke that curled from the holes in oblique clay roofs.

Oqa.

~~~

They told me the carpet was beautiful.

Eagles spread their angular wings in the rhombic flakes of its ultramarine sky and rows of pomegranate trees grew along its fringes. Upon its background, dun like the hide of a camel or like the very sands that ruched past Oqa, almonds lay on maroon platters and lotus flowers bloomed. Its weave fastened Thawra's aches and desires and spells of morning sickness and Hazar Gul's silliness and Boston's arthritic sighs. Leila's hands sticky with candy and her dreams from all the times she had fallen asleep on the loom and drooled on it a little. Choreh Gul's drugged mornings and Zakrullah's famished crying. Down from the chickens that danced upon the carpet when Thawra wasn't looking. Nurullah's temper tantrums and tea dregs and goat turds and specks of gold from the barchan belt. Two hundred and forty symmetrical knots per square inch. Three hundred seventy-two thousand knots per square meter. One million one hundred and sixteen thousand knots in all.

All of that had fit into the pannier of Baba Nazar's donkey perfectly. In Dawlatabad, Abdul Shakur the yarn dealer had run his fingernail against the back of the carpet and studied the pile for mistakes and bought it for two hundred dollars, and then turned around and sold it to a dealer from Mazar for two-twenty.

That was about three weeks after Ramadan. By the time Qasim and Ramin and I hiked up the hummock in the drizzle of November, the loom had been dismantled and the beams put away and the loom room was stocked with dusty pyramids of large burlap sacks stuffed with hay, animal feed for the winter. The carpet was gone.

In its place was a little girl.

Her name was Sahra Gul: Desert Flower. Her face was pink and fat and smooth, and she was healthy, and her eyes were dark and vatic pools. She was born in the month of Mizan, two weeks after Thawra had finished her carpet. Boston midwifed. It was an easy evening birth by lamplight, and the moon had stared away the dust, and the sky was gold-speckled ultramarine. Amanullah was hanging out with some friends at the far side of the village that night. When he returned home, his third child was waiting for him.

He said to his wife: "Oh! You are two people now!"

When I met Sahra Gul, Thawra was holding her against her chest. She had swaddled her daughter in blankets and scarves and old adult clothes ripped into sheets. The weaver herself wore a sweater over her calico dress. Yet through all that cloth she could feel her daughter's little heart go *thk-thk-thk*. Barely visible dimples of affection blossomed on the woman's sunken cheeks.

"Are you going to have more children, Amanullah?" I asked.

"*Inshallah*. I'll accept more."

And he smiled his sly mustachioed smile and his strabismic eyes narrowed with mischief.

＞＞＞＞

Villagers crowded Amanullah's bedroom. They squatted and sat and reclined, and their level of comfort and geography in the room as always corresponded to their status in it. Amin Bai sprawled by the old trousseau at the upper end, catlike and much pleased with my gift of Bushnell binoculars with twelve-power magnification and coated antiglare optics. They were sleek and black and the object of instant admiration by the men, most of all Choreh, who had stridden into the room urgent and high, and clasped my hand hard and slightly threateningly, and held it so for a long time and then said: "Next time, bring me binoculars as well." And he looked me straight in the eye with his tiny frozen pupils, unblinking.

The Oqans were there to trade stories and to drink tea—because it was always good to drink someone else's tea, because there was little else to do, and because their communality offered the villagers a sanctuary, however make-believe, from their stunning and stunningly malign land. Yet an ineffable brokenness blew through the room the way sand blew up the stoss slopes of the lunate dunes outside.

Something was askew about the greenish pallor of Zakrullah's skin, his cavernous cough, his apathetic limbs hanging thin and limp from the left hip of Choreh Gul where she stood in the doorway. About the way Baba Nazar rummaged in his memory for a full minute before thinking of the name of his youngest, seventh grandchild. About the way Leila pranced past the squatting boys and men, and plopped down next to her grandfather, and tucked in her feet, and put a condom in her mouth, and blew it up into a balloon, let the air out, blew it up again, deflated it again, blew it up, repeated. "I'm dizzy I'm dizzy I'm dizzy," she said. No one laughed. A boy maybe twice as old as Leila lit a cigarette in the corner. Baba Nazar shook his head and looked away. Children nowadays.

Next to Baba Nazar sat his nephew, Abed Nazar the soldier, home on leave from deployment in Kunar and trapped in the village by the weather for more than a fortnight. He had brought war to Oqa, on his cell phone. A video of an ambush that killed two American and four Afghan soldiers. A photo of Abed Nazar himself, with a rocket-propelled grenade launcher on the shoulder of his black uniform sweater, posing against the backdrop of the glaucous folds of a distant mountain ridge. A photo of an "American soldier, my friend," squatting over a tin bowl of some kind of frontier chow, his camouflage sleeves rolled up to display colorful tattoos, of which the largest was a red and blue five-point star. Photos of another American soldier eating rice, smiling at the camera, his face sprinkled with acne, and of a third, at rest on a foldout cot under the large camouflage flap of a tent. I had seen such photos. I had been in such tents, in Iraq, in Chechnya. No one got out of them with his soul intact.

"Where do you like it better, Abed *jan*, Oqa or Kunar?"

"Kunar."

"Why?"

"I like war."

The young boys in the room listened with admiration, their mouths half open. Leila had let the air out of the condom and was now chewing on it.

"Every day war, every day war," grumbled Baba Nazar from his spot by the stove.

"What do you think about it, Baba Nazar?" I asked.

"Nothing to think about. It's war. Is war good?"

He opened the door of the *bukhari* and stared at the small hot fire in it and said that three days earlier an airplane had flown over Oqa without a sound. He said it had flown very low.

"Maybe it was a drone," said Abed Nazar, who had seen such things. "Maybe they think Oqa is a Taliban village."

"Well," said Baba Nazar, and closed the stove door again. For a long time he said nothing more. Next to him, the frail and bony Sayed Nafas quietly rolled and rolled between his thumb and forefinger someone's cigarette butt, and the stinking dregs of tobacco from the cartridge flaked down onto Amanullah's bedroom floor.

Baba Nazar asked me to step outside with him. The wind was gusting fifty knots. Thistle skeletons hissed in the desert. From the northern wall of the house flapped the pelt of a desert fox the old hunter had trapped just beneath the hummock the day before. We slipped on wet clay.

"Anna," Baba Nazar said. "We love you. We are glad you came from America to see us. But we have no weapons. We are worried about your security here, and I am worried about my security after you leave."

I thanked him for his kindness and waited for more. A rooster crowed. A couple hundred yards away, the asthmatic Kizil Gul and

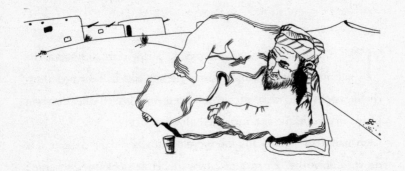

her heroin-addict son, Abdul Rashid, were pitchforking thornbrush in tandem into a lacy wall of fodder. Boston shuffled by with her back straight like a cane. In outstretched hands she carried two loaves of freshly baked *sharbi*, bread kneaded with onions and sheep fat. Steam from her cooking pulsated in the wind like something alive, like a heart.

At length Baba Nazar said: "Anna, I know in the past I have invited you to stay. But I don't think you should spend the night here."

A deep breath, and suddenly I pictured us the way a bird would see us, a white dove cast off course, or a demoiselle crane perhaps halfway on its hallowed and time-and-again desecrated migration across the big slate sky: two people working, a woman carrying food, an importunate visitor, and an old man barefoot in his black galoshes, his glasses held on his head by string, his Soviet shotgun a poor match for the war around him. Five tiny and fragile figures in the sodden desert, a poor man's carpet decocted out of an eternity of violence and generosity and grace. Each of us flawed, and so, complete. All of us woven into a time warp named Oqa.

The weather cleared that afternoon. Wispy cirri slid about the pale and brittle autumn skin of the sky like half-formed afterthoughts. In the west, a cold lusterless sun gilded the Bactrian plains in an antique and tarnished glow.

Amanullah steered his motorcycle into that slanted light. He drove maniacally. He jumped over russet hassocks and charged rusty boulders and skidded on wet smears of ocher clay. He blazed through pink morass and blue puddles where once there had been paths, caromed through patches of slough. He sped up, took narrow irrigation ditches flying, slowed down, sped up again, zigzagged. The wheels of his motorcycle lost traction and regained it and touched off canted fountains of mud that bore bits of human and animal bone and flakes of pottery and fragments of metal and shreds of plastic, and this protean exhibit of Anthropocene specimens propelled past the subdued sunset and splotched back down in rapid-fire arches. I sat astride behind him, clinging to his waist with my one good arm, too scared by our mad flight to do anything but laugh. So I laughed. Amanullah had adjusted his two rearview mirrors to watch my face, and each time I gripped him tighter he would beam and lean back against me as if to lie down on me and go faster still.

Amanullah was fleeing Oqa.

"I will take you to Kabul!" he shouted. "I will take you to Kandahar!"

Two other motorcycles debauched across the desert. Amanullah's friend Asad, who had wrestled with him in the dunes the previous winter, drove Ramin. Qasim rode with Paidi, who was known mostly for having kidnapped a woman from Khairabad betrothed to someone else and marrying her—an immoral thing to have done, everyone agreed, though no one demanded that Paidi be punished for it. It was unclear whether the woman had had any preference one way or another.

The three drivers drag raced over gulches and gloppy fields and barren pastures, and whooped and careened into the wind. Loud and twitching psychotic circus riders reenacting the millennial bacchanal reckless men had performed upon this land since time immemorial, horseback and camelback and in tanks.

We could barely skylight in the south the quiet calligraphy of Karaghuzhlah's naked orchards and breast-shaped clay roofs when the riders rumbled to a halt. An irrigation canal too deep and too wide for motorcycles to cross. A moat around Amanullah's vagabond dreams.

We dismounted. Ramin and Qasim and I would walk the last two miles to Karaghuzhlah, spend the night, drive on south. But not Amanullah. Amanullah would have to ride back to Oqa.

Stuck, again.

"Well," he said, and the rest of us shuffled in the slippery mud and repeated: "Well."

Amanullah took a couple of long steps through the muck and stood astride the ditch, one foot on each loamy bank, facing west. Between his legs slow murky bubbles formed and burst upon a mocha-colored current that carried humus to thirsty fields. He beckoned to me. Then he grabbed me by the waist and lifted me up into the air and held me there long enough to give me three wet kisses on the cheeks and placed me on the southern side of the dike. Qasim and Ramin jumped across. Amanullah pushed himself off with his left foot and scrambled up the northern bank.

We stood on either side of the ditch and held our cold right hands to our hearts in the age-old gesture of gratitude and affection, of greeting and farewell. The sun had pitched its scarlet yurt in the west, where beyond Dawlatabad and Andkhoi and Turkmenistan and Iran, beyond an unfordable ocean, unreachable by donkey, lay America. To the south, evening dogs were barking, and boys were whipping the last sheep home from pasture through the clanging sheetmetal gates of Karaghuzhlah, and the wind carried ribbons of muezzins' amplified calls like a salve to the desert. To the east, a purple darkness was spreading above the snow-streaked copper mountains. In a few hours a lidded waning moon would rise upon that dark curtain, and the Milky Way would follow, bisecting the sky, resplendent.

"Afghanistan is our country, Anna. It can be your country, too," Amanullah called to me across the ditch. And then, out of the blue, caked up to his shins in Khorasan mud, he declaimed a rendition of Rumi's most famous verse.

"So that you can come, yet again, come, come to our house."

For his was a country of poets.

> It doesn't matter if you have broken your vow
> A thousand times. Come,
> Yet again, come, come.

Oqa lay somewhere to the northeast. A village unmapped, un-remembered, unaccounted for. We could not see it from the ditch. But it was there, and Amanullah would never escape from it. In the spring, when winter wheat would rise above the knee in the rain-slaked fields of Balkh, Amanullah and Baba Nazar would ride to Dawlatabad and buy skeins of yarn that would smell like sweat and sheep dung and lamb fat and juniper smoke, and bring them to the village. Boston would roll the yarn into balls. Leila would fasten pale warps to the rusty beams, and Thawra would hang Sahra Gul's woven cradle over her loom and tie the first knot of her next carpet. In a year or two, two or three million knots later, Leila would join her, and then Sahra Gul. They would weave their foremothers' lotus blossoms and their kinsmen's wars, the golden eagles of their desert, the music of their village and its silences, its weddings and funerals, their own joys and sorrows. They would sever the yarn with old sweat-stained sickles in time with the sacrosanct rhythm of their hearts. On the edge of a sand-dune sea, on the edge of a war zone, in their crepuscular loom room on the edge of the world, past and present would converge.

ACKNOWLEDGMENTS

Research in Afghanistan was supported by a grant from the Pulitzer Center on Crisis Reporting. The author also thanks Becky Saletan and Felicia Eth for helping to make this book a reality.

She is indebted to generations of storytellers whose wisdom kept her company and lent her compass bearings in the desert. A friend kept track of her on the map and helped replenish her bookshelves. Thank you. You were a muse.

To her Afghan hosts and fellow travelers, who made her family and risked their lives to protect hers, she bows deeply, with profound respect. This book is for you.

ANNA BADKHEN has been writing about development, conflict, and people in extremis around the world since 2000 for the *San Francisco Chronicle*, the *New Republic*, *Foreign Policy*, and the *Boston Globe*, among others. She has reported from the Middle East, Central Asia, East Africa, and her native Russia and the Caucasus. Her wartime reporting won the 2007 Joel R. Seldin Award from Psychologists for Social Responsibility. The author of *Peace Meals* and other nonfiction books, she lives in Philadelphia.